Outdo
for the

4/04

DATE DUE		
MAR 17	AUG 18 00	
MAY 01	NOV 02 00	
JUN 13	JUL 07 2003	
JUL 21		
NOV 30		
JUL 11 1996		
JUN 05 '97		
OCT 24 '97		
MAY 11 '98		
JUN 24 '98		
OCT 20 '98		
DEC 31 '98		

Outdoor Projects for the Country Home

Peter Badger

TAB Books
Division of McGraw-Hill, Inc.
Blue Ridge Summit, PA 17294-0850

FIRST EDITION
FIRST PRINTING

© 1993 by **TAB Books**.
TAB Books is a division of McGraw-Hill, Inc.

Library of Congress Cataloging-in-Publication Data
Badger, Peter.
    Outdoor projects for the country home / by Peter Badger.
        p.   cm.
    Includes index.
    ISBN 0-8306-4399-0 (pbk.)
    1. Rustic woodwork.   I. Title.
TT200.B33   1993
674´.8—dc20   92-45742
                                                                      CIP

Acquisitions Editor: Stacy Varavvas-Pomeroy
Book Editor: April D. Nolan
Production team: Katherine G. Brown, Director
                Brenda M. Plasterer, Layout
                Jana L. Fisher, Coding
                Susan E. Hansford, Coding
                Brenda M. Plasterer, Coding
                Janice Stottlemyer, Computer Illustrator
                Ruth Gunnett, Computer Illustrator
                Tara Ernst, Proofreading
                Stacey R. Spurlock, Indexer
Design team: Jaclyn J. Boone, Designer
                Brian Allison, Associate Designer
Cover design and illustration: Sandra Blair, Harrisburg, Pa

HT1

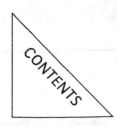
CONTENTS

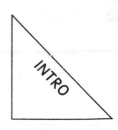

WOODWORKING AND HOMESTEADING GO TOGETHER; they easily complement each other. If you are already an enthusiastic woodworker setting up a home in the country, you will find plenty of opportunities for using your skill with wood. Even if you are not yet a keen woodworker, a country home can give you the chance to learn how to use wood in circumstances where extreme accuracy is not as important as if you were making household furniture. You do not need cabinetmaking skills to do the many woodworking jobs that will improve your country property, nor do you need a very extensive kit of tools.

If your country home has only enough land for a modest garden, or if it extends to many acres of varied land, you can make a large variety of things that will improve your use and enjoyment of your place in the country. Besides the enjoyment that comes from the work you do, you also will save money—often a considerable amount compared with paying someone else to build what you want or buying items ready-made.

This book offers a range of projects you can make for use on or about your property. No doubt many of these designs will suggest other ideas. Having a country home gives you almost unlimited scope for making things, all of which can only increase both the convenience and value of the land and what is on it. However, keep in mind that this book stops short at the door of your house. There are many other books dealing with furniture and other things to make for use indoors.

To make the best use of the book, look through all the notes and instructions, even if you have no immediate need for a particular project. Each project contains descriptions of techniques that could be of value in projects you devise yourself. If some terms are new to you, you should find their meaning in the glossary. In the materials lists and drawings, all sizes are in inches unless marked differently.

Wood sources & preparation

IF YOU HAVE A PIECE OF COUNTRY PROPERTY you wish to
develop, whether it is a large garden or more extensive land
with meadows and woodland, you will want to plan ahead
what you intend to do. Your first ideas might not be your final
ones, so try not to rush into alterations and new construction.
Allow yourself some time to ponder.

You might do some work on your property with stones,
concrete slabs, and bricks, probably coupled with concrete. You
might use compacted soil or mud. If your land is very stony,
you might be glad to dig stones for walls, to serve as paths,
fences, or foundations for buildings. However, for most
homesteaders or country dwellers with some land to till or on
which to keep animals, the common constructional material is
wood, and that is what mainly concerns the contents of this
book.

Although this book is about woodworking, what you do with
wood has to fit in with other developments, so think of it in
relation to the whole scene. If you are too enthusiastic, you
might go ahead with new construction and possibly wish later
you had done it some other way. Fortunately, much of the
development of your property can probably be done with wood,
and you can work it with a few tools. Skill gained by practice
with the tools and materials described in the following pages
should allow you to achieve the results you want.

The trees growing on your land are possible sources of wood for
some of your projects. There is certainly an attraction about
using wood from your own trees, but think hard about it before
you attack a tree with a chain saw or ax. Felling is final; you
cannot change your mind.

Your own trees

Keep in mind, too, the effect of harvesting your own trees in regard to the rest of your property. Trees improve the appearance of your land, act as windbreaks, provide shade, and shelter animals. Will the loss of trees affect these considerations?

Trees are a crop not unlike any other you might cultivate on your property, but their life cycle is extremely long. Even the quickest-growing softwood (coniferous tree) takes 20 years to grow to a useful size, and hardwoods (the broad-leafed trees) could take five times that long. It might be your children, not you, who fell the second crop.

Selective thinning

When selecting trees to convert to wood, look at the possibility of thinning dense woodland to get long, straight trunks. Trees close together compete with each other to get upward to the light, so they grow tall and develop branches only near their tops. This gives clear wood in most of the trunk, which is the most useful source of wood from trees.

Tree management can be more important than getting what you want quickly, regardless of what is left. If you remove trees here and there, the remaining trees will have space to develop. In coming years, they will be larger and possibly more useful to you as you thin again.

What to look for

Because it is the trunk of a tree that yields most useful wood, assess what you can expect from it. Large branches might be useful for some projects, but mostly they will become bean sticks and firewood. If there are branches starting low on the tree, you can expect a great many knots in the trunk. Knots might not matter if you plan to use the trunk as a round post, but if you plan to cut the trunk into boards, the knots could weaken and disfigure the wood.

As a tree grows it forms rings each year from the center outward. If you cut across a log, you can tell the age of the tree by counting the *annual rings*, which are more easily seen in most hardwoods than in some softwoods. The grain toward the center is the denser *heartwood*, which is stronger and more durable. The newer *sapwood*, found toward the outside, is weaker and more liable to rot and to attract boring insects.

If you cut a log into boards, you should trim off any sapwood that is obvious by its lighter color. In some softwoods, though, all wood looks the same, and you can use almost the whole width.

You should remove bark, if possible, from any wood you intend to use, even if you won't use it for some time. A few species of trees have bark that is very firmly attached and will have to be left, but most bark can be lifted and peeled with a tool. Bark harbors harmful insects, and you will find the undersurface wet with sap, which has to be dried from the wood. After you peel it from the tree, save the bark. Broken into small pieces, bark makes an excellent mulch for the garden

What to avoid

Look warily at a tree growing in isolation; it might be better left to provide shade for you or for animals. If you weigh up what you might get out of it in useful wood, the result could show that it is not worth felling for its usable wood. The low branches of an isolated tree will mean many, possibly large knots.

In addition, you are unlikely to be able to split wood from a tree grown in isolation because winds will have caused the tree to have a twisted and bent trunk. Such a trunk might produce interesting grain patterns for a furniture maker, but its wood is of little use to an outdoor woodworker.

A tree that has swung in winds might develop *shakes*, or lengthwise separations in the grain resulting in cracks. Some are not apparent until the wood starts to dry. Providing they are not large, shakes will not affect the strength of the wood when used as a post or pole, but they would not be acceptable in furniture.

Seasoning

The lifeblood of a tree is the sap that rises and falls within it. You will find less sap in wood from trees felled in the winter than at other times, but there will always be too much moisture in newly felled wood for it to be satisfactory

Wood sources & preparation 3

immediately for any important purpose. Wood containing sap is called *green* (which has nothing to do with its color). Reducing the amount of sap to an acceptable level is called *seasoning*.

As the sap dries out, the wood will shrink and it might warp. Shrinkage is across the grain; reduction in length is negligible. If you use green wood for a field fence, subsequent shrinkage or warping of rails might not matter. However, if you use green wood to make a wall, what were closely fitting boards could shrink to leave wide gaps. Even worse, such boards used for a floor could result in a warped, uneven surface.

If you buy wood from a lumberyard, it should be already seasoned and ready for use. Even then it is worthwhile to buy it a month or more in advance of your needs so you can allow the wood to dry more and settle to a stable condition.

It is impossible—and unnecessary—to drive out all moisture. When there is only a low moisture content, the wood stabilizes by giving out and taking up moisture in balance with the surrounding air. Almost all bought wood is seasoned by a special, fast method (unavailable to you) that dries out moisture until what remains does not affect the wood. On your own property, the only way of seasoning is the traditional method of letting the wood dry naturally. The accepted rule is to allow 1 year for every 1 inch of thickness. The thinner the wood, then, the quicker the seasoning—but even thin wood takes a long time to "dry."

How to season your own wood

Cut your wood into boards or have a sawmill do it, leaving a little more than you want the final thickness to be. Stack the boards with spacers, called *stickers*, so air can circulate. (This process, called *stickering the boards*, is shown on next page.)

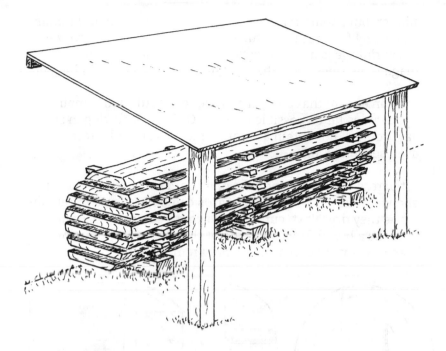

Protect the boards from sun and rain, preferably with a roof of some sort, but do not include walls or anything else that will restrict movement of air. To prevent the ends from drying too quickly and possibly causing splits, paint over the end grain.

The economical way to cut a log is with all cuts straight across, called *through and through*.

Cutting

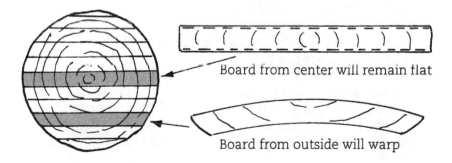

Board from center will remain flat

Board from outside will warp

Possible warping as the wood shrinks during drying out can be forecast. A board that crosses the center of the log will get thinner, but should remain flat. Those next to it should remain reasonably flat, but those further out can be expected to warp. The shrinkage is in the direction of the annual rings, so if you imagine the rings trying to straighten, that is what will happen.

You can ensure that a larger number of boards will remain flat if you cut as far as possible radially. Of course, cutting in such a way, you will not obtain as many or as wide boards from a given section of log.

Cut across the center and take one board each side of the cut (shown far left). These broad boards can be expected to remain flat as they dry. Next, cut the two semicircular pieces in half, and take a board from each side of the cut, as shown below. These narrower boards, too, should remain flat.

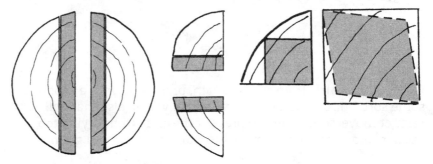

What you do with the last pieces depends on their size, but you can cut more pieces or probably make squares, as shown above Although you might cut a true square from a quadrant of the log, when it has seasoned it will have shrunk most in the direction of the annual rings to a diamond section shown above at far right. If you need an exact square, you will have to machine the piece again.

Any seasoning of round posts or balks of wood that are cut by squaring a log will have to be only partial. You do not want to wait for years, but you should leave the wood as long as possible for at least an initial drying before using the wood.

You can speed up the seasoning process with heat. Dry heat in an oven will hasten the process, but obviously this only suits small pieces of wood, unless you can improvise a very large oven.

Woods vary considerably in their durability when used outdoors, especially when in contact with soil. Some contain natural resins that act as preservatives. Other woods will not last long if used outdoors and untreated. A few hardwoods can be expected to have a long life when exposed, but many that are sought after for indoor furniture quickly succumb to rot, mold, borers, and the effect of weather if used outside. There are some long-lasting oaks, but others—together with ash, beech, birch, and maple—will not last long outdoors if untreated.

The common building softwoods need to be treated with preservative if they are to have much life in an outdoor structure. Some softwoods are very resinous and naturally resistant to insects and molds. California redwood, cedar, and cypress could last untreated for at least a couple of decades. If you have any of these trees on your property, they are worth converting to make the structures you need; they are usually very expensive to buy.

Among the most durable forms of wood obtainable today for outdoor use is *pressure-treated lumber,* called *PT* in the trade. It is construction-quality softwood, and it may be Southern yellow pine or Douglas fir. The wood is saturated throughout with a preservative so it is completely protected against rot, borers, and other attack. If you buy pressure-treated wood and use it as it is, there are no health problems. However, if you want to alter sizes by putting the treated wood through a table saw or planer, you should realize that working with pressure-treated lumber can present certain health risks.

The most common and dangerous preservatives are ammonium copper arsenate and chromated copper arsenate. If the wood you obtain has a greenish tinge, it probably has a high copper content from one of these chemicals. (As the wood ages, the color will weather to gray.) Dust created while working this wood can enter your lungs and contaminate your skin either directly or by lodging in your clothing. Brief exposure to the dust will irritate your throat, eyes, and skin. Longer exposure can result in dermatitis, bronchitis, nerve damage, and other effects.

If you are working the wood outdoors and can avoid most of the dust, there is little risk when doing brief machining. For more prolonged work, though—particularly in a confined space—you should take precautions. Ideally, your shop will have dust-extraction equipment. You should wear a fitted respirator—not a paperlike mask. Ideally, you should also wear goggles to prevent the dust from causing irritation in your eyes.

Preserving your own wood

There is no way you can apply preservative yourself that will achieve penetration as thorough as pressure-treating. The nearest you can get is soaking wood for a prolonged period in a preservative. In many circumstances, you would not regard that as justified, but if the wood is a suitable size for you to fit it in a tank or trough filled with preservative, you can allow soaking for several days. You might be able to soak just the parts that will be in contact with the earth. For example, you could soak just the bottoms of posts in a bucket and treat the other parts by brushing.

You can buy brush-on preservative under various trade names, and, although you won't get much penetration, several coats of this will provide protection for a reasonable time. End grain is most vulnerable to rot and is also most absorbent, so use plenty of preservative there. Besides applying preservative you can reduce the risk of rot caused by covering end grain completely, such as by putting a capping on the top of a fence post.

Besides the commercially available preservatives, you might find others cheaper and equally effective, if rather messy. Creosote has a long history as a wood preservative. You can use it for soaking or brushing. Several brushed coats every few days should be effective. Tar, applied hot, might not penetrate much, but it puts on a waterproof, protective coat that is particularly effective for the part of a post that will be buried in the ground.

Oil and water do not mix, so if you can penetrate wood with oil, it will repel water and, therefore, reduce the risk of rot. A treatment that has negligible cost is soaking softwood in used automobile oil. This is particularly appropriate if you cut softwood posts on your own property and strip bark from them. It is a slow process, so you must plan ahead and build up a stock of treated posts in anticipation of your needs.

Cover the posts with oil in a trough and leave them for about two months. Remove the posts and put them on a rack to drain and dry. All this can be messy, so devise some sort of tongs or hook to lift the posts and arrange strips of wood or metal above or close to the trough for drying.

Charring is a traditional way of dealing with post ends that costs nothing and gives limited protection against rot. To char, make a wood fire and hold all of the end of a post that will be buried in the flame. Move it around so all the surface is evenly burned black. A thin layer should be reduced to a black dust.

Whatever the method of preservation used, consider the effect on stock and vegetation. Once any preservative has dried for a few days it should not be dangerous to animals—unless any of them chew wood! There should be no effect on vegetation, although it might be advisable to keep vegetables or important flowers away from pressure-treated wood that might leach poisonous chemicals into the soil.

Salvaged wood

With recycling so much in the forefront of our social conscience, you might think seriously about reusing wood as you make things for your property. Salvaged wood can come from many sources. You might take apart old buildings and structures on your property, or you might have neighbors who would be more than glad to have you disassemble and remove wooden buildings on their property.

Watchpoints for "recycling" wood

One advantage of using wood obtained by disassembling something old is that there is no doubt about it being seasoned. Natural seasoning will have happened if your wood has been built into something for a long time.

Parts of old assemblies might be rotten, so keep in mind that, because spores of rot are carried in the air, nearby sound wood might be affected, too. Before you bring home salvaged wood, cut away any rotten wood and burn it. To be safe from the possible onset of rot, a piece of wood with a rotten end should be cut off 2 feet past the last evidence of rot.

Carefully separate parts of an old assembly to avoid splits. Where there does not seem much chance of extracting nails to keep the wood sound, it might be better to saw alongside the joint. You get shorter wood, but it will be sound instead of broken.

If possible, identify the old wood. If the wood has been varnished or polished and you can see the grain pattern, you should be able to get some idea of the type of wood. This will help you in deciding if it is suitable for your new project.

A wood's previous use can guide you, too. For example, if it was furniture, it is almost certainly hardwood, while much of the wood used for structures of buildings or cladding is softwood. Posts, or anything else driven into the ground, might be untreated hardwood or softwood treated with preservative. In general, hardwoods are heavier than softwoods; some very much so.

Wood previously used for indoor furniture or for the internal parts of a house should certainly be good for a new life in something you make for indoor or outdoor use. Much wood previously used outside can have a further life, if only in cruder outside structures and equipment. Some wood weathered extensively outside might still have a worthwhile center. For instance, a 4-inch-square length of a durable hardwood might look very bad outside, yet it could cut down to a sound 2-inch-square internal piece. It is a good idea to build up a stock of previously used wood, even if you can see no immediate need for it. Most of it is not yet due to be used as firewood, a fate from which there is no return.

Other sources of used wood

Crates and pallets are used for many things and often discarded. Pallets are reused until, perhaps, just one board breaks; then they are scrapped. You can recover useful wood from the remainder, usually with fairly easy disassembly.

Machinery and some bigger domestic appliances are often crated. These boxes are of mixed construction, but most will yield some useful wood, even if you have to scrap a few parts. Imported machinery crates are a good source. These crates are nonreturnable and an importer might be glad to let you take away what he would otherwise burn. The exporter, usually in an eastern country, uses local wood, and you might find yourself with pieces of mahogany, or other more valuable wood, that might be suitable for furniture.

Plywood for most projects on your property should be waterproof. To be sure of that, you need exterior- or marine-grade. Most plywood is now bonded with waterproof glue, but you should suspect salvaged plywood, particularly from imported crates and boxes, to be of inferior quality. Plywood from this source was intended only to survive one trip, and it will probably disintegrate if it is subjected to heavy rain. You certainly would be disappointed if you built it into an outdoor project and the panels delaminated.

Salvaging other materials

In pioneer days, nails were more valuable than wood, so old assemblies were burned for the sake of recovering the nails, which were not affected by fire. Today, large nails are comparatively expensive, so you might consider doing the same with waste wood.

New wood

You will almost certainly have to buy some new wood. When you do, go to the lumberyard with a detailed list. You might save money by accepting offcuts. Short pieces cut from other orders might suit your needs. If you want two 6-foot lengths, remember that asking for one 12-foot length will cost more. In addition, try not to be too demanding about sections of wood; you might be able to use stock sections.

Look over the wood on offer. As a natural product, pieces of wood will differ. If you are asked to accept wood with many knots and shakes (if such wood would be good enough for your purposes), expect a special price.

If you go to a sawmill, where wood is cut from logs, instead of to a lumberyard, where wood is bought already cut to size, ask what happens to the pieces cut from the outsides of logs. Boards are first cut so that at least one edge follows the contour of the outside of the log. That *waney* edge is then cut off to make a parallel board. Ask what happens to those pieces. You might get a truckload free or at firewood prices. Some of it will be firewood, but other pieces make useful battens and even larger strips.

Wood from a lumberyard will be already seasoned, but even then it is worthwhile storing the wood for a few weeks in the atmosphere where it is expected to be used. Some might warp or twist and have to be discarded or cut for something different from the original purpose.

Softwoods, such as the many varieties of spruce and fir, nearly all of which bear needles, grow comparatively quickly. You will probably find most use for these trees in making posts or poles, although some will split for fence rails. The broadleaf hardwoods, with their long growing period, can produce long-lasting poles from tall trees, but most hardwoods are useful cut into boards.

Sizes

If you buy new wood, make yourself familiar with stock sizes. Many are spoken of as "2 by," meaning the section is 2 inches by some other standard size. Check your local stockist. He might favor certain standard sizes and could even have an excess of one section selling cheaply. Avoid planning some structure with odd sections of wood and then finding you have to pay extra to have it machined from a standard section.

Standard sizes are for sawn wood. If you want the wood planed, it will be about ¼ inch undersize. What is sold as 2-inch-by-4-inch wood (standard size) will actually be 1¾-inch-by-3¾-inch wood when bought planed (*nominal size*).

If you want several pieces of the same section that total 20 feet, do not ask for a 20-foot piece. Take along your cutting list. If what you want can be found among short pieces, you should pay less and have less of a transport problem.

Stock sizes are usual with construction-quality softwood. With hardwoods, particularly the less-common ones, sizes depend on availability. Narrow pieces should be cheaper than wide ones. Because of tree sizes, you might not be able to get wide boards in some woods. Be prepared to glue if you must make wide pieces. Several modern glues are weatherproof.

Manufactured boards

Much indoor furniture and similar woodwork today is constructed mainly of manufactured boards, which are perfectly suitable for that purpose—yet unsuitable for use outside.

Hardboard, even the oil-tempered type, will disintegrate in a short time if exposed to the weather. You might find limited use for hardboard inside one of your outbuildings, but it is best avoided on a homestead.

Particleboard, whether faced or not, does not stand up to moisture, which gets into a panel, swells the wood chips, and distorts the whole thing to destruction. If kept dry and under cover, particleboard is a convenient material in uniform, flat pieces, but it needs care in garden and homestead use.

Plywood

Most plywood today is bonded with water-resistant glue, but for outdoor use, you should use only plywood graded as *exterior* or *marine*. There are several qualities, mainly defined according to the number of knots and the condition of surfaces. Many woods are used to make plywood, but the most commonly available and suitable for outdoor use is Douglas fir exterior plywood. Stock-size sheets are 48 inches by 96 inches, in many thicknesses. You should find that ½-inch-thick pieces will suit most of your needs.

Keep in mind that the price of plywood should not be vastly different from what it would cost to buy enough solid wood to cover the same area. Of course, with solid wood, you do not have the benefit of an unbroken, impenetrable surface.

Construction workers use a large amount of exterior-grade plywood to make forms for concrete work. Much of this is discarded after one use, and you might be able to obtain some of this still-usable plywood at little or no cost.

Planning & development

PLANNING AHEAD IS IMPORTANT. Much of the difference between a professional and an amateur is the time taken on a job. For the professional, time is money and work is planned so it is tackled as efficiently as possible. You might be tackling similar work because you enjoy it and are not in a great hurry, but even then you could be frustrated by inefficiency.

Think through a project. As far as possible, know what you have to do at every step. Not only that; know what materials and tools you will require. For the projects in this book, steps are described and materials lists are provided. As you progress, try always to know the step after the next.

Use your time efficiently and plan each working session so you have all you need ready for use. It can be annoying to have to stop and waste time going to the store for more of something, like a certain size of nail.

Part of thinking ahead is anticipating what has to be done to a particular piece of wood. Besides the work you are presently doing, there might be other operations that would be easier to do now than after the wood is built into another part. While you have a piece of wood on the bench or trestles for cutting joints, you could also drill holes that will be needed at a later stage and possibly plane off what will be exposed edges. Prefabrication as far as possible saves time and is often easier to do accurately.

Economic concerns

Part of your planning should be economic buying. If you expect to be tackling several projects, even if they will be spread over a long period, it should be cheaper to buy enough of some things in quantity to cover future needs. Nails are cheaper in bulk. Plywood is cheaper by the sheet than in a cut piece. Paint can be much cheaper in big containers. If you know you will be needing more of some sections of wood, it is satisfying to know you have a stock to draw on. Nails and screws of many sizes are always good stock.

Providing you can afford it, buy more than you need immediately of commonly used items. You will have the backing of a useful stock that will mark you as a regular craftsperson and not just a D-I-Y enthusiast who spends much of his time at a store buying what he needs in expensive small quantities.

Besides what gets built into a project, remember there are other consumable items. Hacksaw and jigsaw blades have to be replaced. Make sure you always have spares. Abrasive paper wears out and a packet might be a better investment than odd sheets. Glue is cheaper in quantity, but check shelf life and make sure you will be able to use the quantity you buy.

Development

If your land is undulating, it will have an attractive appearance because small hills and valleys are more pleasing to the eye than flat land. However, if you want to cultivate your land, it will be easier to work if it is flat. For gardening, you might want to level a plot; that, in turn, could affect any building or fencing planned for it.

It is important that all upright parts are vertical. You cannot shape something to conform to uneven land. Fence posts square to a sloping surface would not look right, and a building erected the same way would look even worse.

The rails of a fence could follow moderately sloping ground, but the posts should be vertical. On a steep slope you might find it better to arrange rail sections in steps, so they are horizontal, as described in the first project (beginning on page 38). Erecting fencing does not usually involve doing anything to the ground except making holes.

If you include a gate, you again have to deal with the ground. On a slope, a gate out of square would not look right, and you would have difficulty getting it to swing properly. If possible, include a gate in a fence where that part of the ground is reasonably level. Otherwise, you must level the ground in the gateway and as far as the gate is to swing. You might also need to modify access slopes in the approach to the gateway, so quite a lot of digging could be necessary.

Levels are even more important if you want to erect a building. The state of the terrain might affect your choice of a position for a building. In a gateway you might be able to estimate a level. However, with the base or foundations for a building, you will need to use a spirit level on a long, straight board because you will have to be as accurate as possible. Even an apparently level field might be a few inches out in the length of a shed. If there is much of a slope, you will have a choice of building into the side of a hill, building up the outer end of the base, or compromising with excavated soil from the back used to build up the front.

Finally, always take into consideration the effect your construction will have on the rest of your property. It helps to be able to see the big picture well before your work begins than to have to live with unsatisfactory results after you have invested your hard-earned time and money.

Tools & techniques

YOU CANNOT DO WOODWORK OF ANY SORT WITHOUT
TOOLS, but for making things on country property you might
not need as many as you expected. If you have had experience
in other branches of woodwork, such as furniture-making or
general carpentry, you can make use of the tools you have. If
you have a shop equipped with power tools, you will find uses
for them, as well. Whatever woodworking tools you have, they
will be useful, but that does not mean all are essential. It's up
to you to decide what tools (and expenses) are justified.

You must weigh up the relative advantages of power and hand
tools. If you consider cost, you can get a lot of hand tools for
the price of one power tool. Electric power tools are mostly only
suitable for use in or near your shop (or near some other power
point). If you have to work farther away you need hand tools.
On an extensive property, would it be justified to buy hand and
power tools for the same purpose? A cordless electric drill of
adequate capacity is an exception that you will probably
consider a good buy, as it can be used anywhere.

If you will be felling trees and cutting up your own logs, a chain
saw is a power tool you will regard as essential. If you hope to
convert the logs you cut into boards, you need a large circular
saw, possibly powered by a gasoline engine. Is that justified, or
would it be more sensible to get the wood converted at a sawmill?

Many power tools are intended for shop use only. Table saws
and planers need to be fairly large if they are to be of value in
this sort of woodwork. A portable circular saw, too, has only
limited use unless it is large. The value of power tools generally
is in doing work faster and with less effort than hand tools. For
work with wood that is already cut to the correct section, you
should be able to do almost everything with hand tools.

You will have your own ideas about the choice of tools to suit
your circumstances, but the following notes are offered as a
guide, both to selecting the most appropriate tools for the job

and to being economical. Two final thoughts on economy: Remember that several tools can have dual purposes, and some can be made or improvised rather than bought.

You will need certain tools on almost every job.

General tools

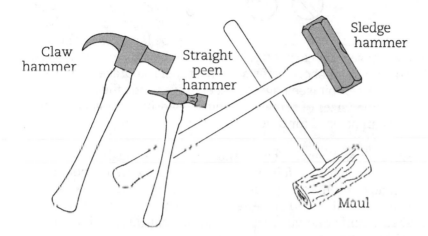

Claw hammer

Straight peen hammer

Sledge hammer

Maul

To drive nails or knocking parts together, pick a claw hammer of a weight you can comfortably manage, probably 16 ounces. The claw can be used for prizing things as well as for pulling nails. Another hammer, about 12 ounces, will do lighter work, and you will find a straight peen useful because it will get into awkward places. You might be glad to have a 7-pound sledge hammer, although most of its work can be done with a maul; you can make one yourself by putting a handle on a log.

Get large pincers with a broad head; these will be helpful in extracting large nails, and they also can serve as wire strainers. Cutting pliers, far right, will pull small nails and wire and can hold many small things. Insulated handles add comfort.

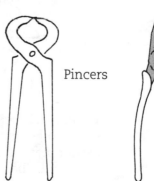

Pincers

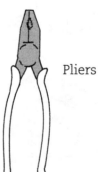

Pliers

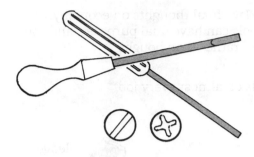

Have several plain screwdrivers of different sizes and some to suit socket-head screws. Avoid ratchet and other special types. Make sure handles will give a good twisting grip. Many of the screws you drive will be larger than those used in general carpentry. You will get best torque with a long driver. For stubborn screws the best tool is a brace with a screwdriver bit (see page 29). Keep driver ends filed to fit particular sizes of screws. A long screwdriver is a good lever and can be used for other things besides driving screws.

Have several pencils, softer than usual. For rough wood it will be better to have a felt-tip marker. A knife with a good point can do exact marking. You can use the type with disposable blades, but it would be better value to have a good clasp or sheath knife that you also can use for whittling and much other cutting.

Measuring tools

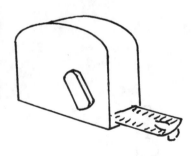

Distances are best measured with an expanding tape rule that extends to at least 12 feet. If you have straight rules or rolled tapes, you will use them, but you need not buy them specially. You can measure long distances with any length of synthetic cord—except nylon, which stretches. Make a loop in the end and tie knots at 6-foot intervals.

Loop   Knots

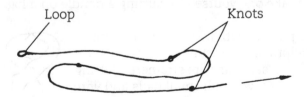

You will find such a measuring cord useful for spacing fence posts or other long distances and, in combination with a tape rule, for measuring intermediate distances from one of the knots in the cord. The extended cord also gives you a straight line.

Another use for cord is to set out a square corner. Start with the knowledge that, in a triangle with sides in the proportion 3:4:5, the corner between the short sides is a right angle. Sizes to mark the cord will depend on your need, but for the foundation of a small building you could mark the cord with loops at 9 feet, 12 feet, and 15 feet.

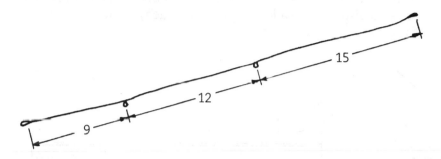

Peg one of the intermediate loops where the corner is to be. Peg the end loops together at a point on the baseline, with the shorter one pulled tight. Extend both remaining parts and peg the other intermediate loop. The short part will be square to the baseline.

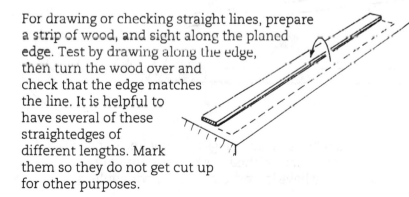

For drawing or checking straight lines, prepare a strip of wood, and sight along the planed edge. Test by drawing along the edge, then turn the wood over and check that the edge matches the line. It is helpful to have several of these straightedges of different lengths. Mark them so they do not get cut up for other purposes.

For marking square across wood you can make a triangle from plywood, shown below to left. You can assume that the corner of a new sheet of plywood is square. Test your square by pressing it against the edge of a piece of wood, draw a line, then flip it over and see if it matches. If you buy a tool for this function, get a combination square, below to right. Besides being a 90° and 45° square, it has ruled markings, and most squares also include a level. The sliding head allows you to use the tool as a gauge with a pencil.

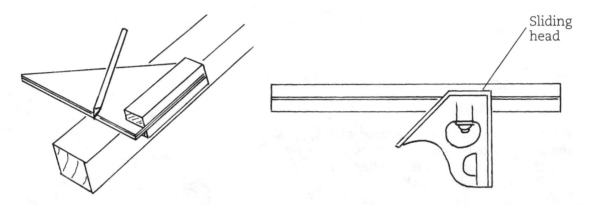

Sliding
head

Saws For cutting by hand what might otherwise be done with a chain saw, you will need a bow saw.

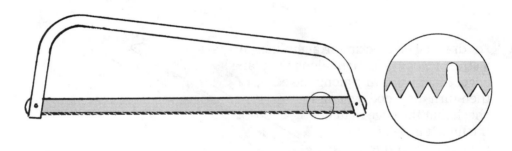

It will cut branches and small logs and any unseasoned wood, but it is too coarse for finished work. The blades are replaceable; they have large teeth, usually with gullets at intervals to clear chip.

You'll need a hand saw for general cutting of seasoned wood, even if you possess a portable circular saw.

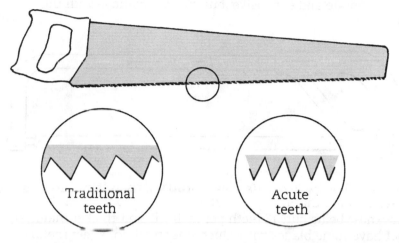

Traditional teeth

Acute teeth

The traditional saw has teeth cut at 60° and can be sharpened with a triangular file. You can now get saws with hardened, more acute teeth, such as the ones shown, which will work for a long time, but then have to be replaced.

General-duty hand saws have teeth spaced at about 8 per inch. For detailed accurate work, as when cutting joints, you need a back or tenon saw, probably with teeth about 14 per inch. It is a good idea to protect the teeth with a slit piece of wood tied onto the saw's blade.

You will have to saw metal, even if it is only cutting off the ends of bolts or bringing a rod to length. Some hacksaw frames are elaborate and expensive, but you can manage with the simplest.

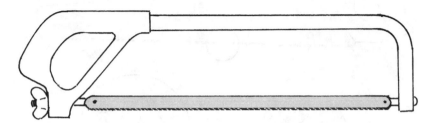

It's advisable to buy spare blades with different teeth spacing. Keep in mind that there should be at least two teeth in the thickness being cut: 18 teeth per inch will suit thicker material, but have some blades with much finer teeth for sheet metals.

Edge tools Unless your work is the crudest hammer-and-nail carpentry, you will need chisels and at least one plane, as well as a means of sharpening them. The range of these tools you obtain will depend on what you intend to do, but for outdoor work you will not need as many cutting tools as you would for work inside the home. Start with the basics suggested and add to them if you find it necessary.

Cheap tools are unlikely to retain cutting edges as long as more expensive ones, so look for a brand name. Plain *firmer* or *butt* chisels are all you need (see page 25, on left side). Bevel-edged ones (see page 25, on right side) can get into corners, but they are not as strong for heavy work. Handles today are usually plastic molded on, so be sure the plastic is strong enough to withstand hitting. Start with ½-inch and 1-inch chisels, then get others if you need them. Special-purpose chisels and gouges might be tempting, but make sure you really need them before you spend the money.

A hand plane will deal with edges, smooth ends, and level surfaces. However, when dealing with oversized pieces (as you often will be in this kind of work), if you want a large area planed, it is better to buy the wood already planed or put it through some sort of power planer. A suitable hand plane to start with is a steel smoothing plane, such as a Stanley #4.

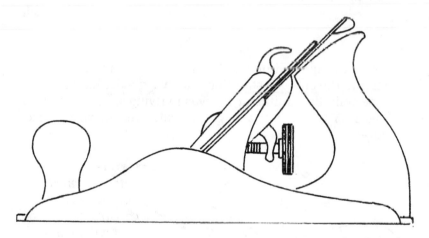

If you already have other planes, you will find uses for them, but the smoothing plane can be adjusted for different woods and degrees of cut. In any case, do not expect to have much success with a plane on wood that is still full of sap.

Axes and hatchets combine cutting with a wedge action. Their edges should be kept sharp. What use you make of them depends on the work you anticipate. You might feel happier with wedges for splitting, driven with a hammer. You can work along a log with three steel wedges, opening the split progressively, then taking the first wedge past the others to drive again, and so on. Using wedges allows for more precision than swinging an ax for the same effect.

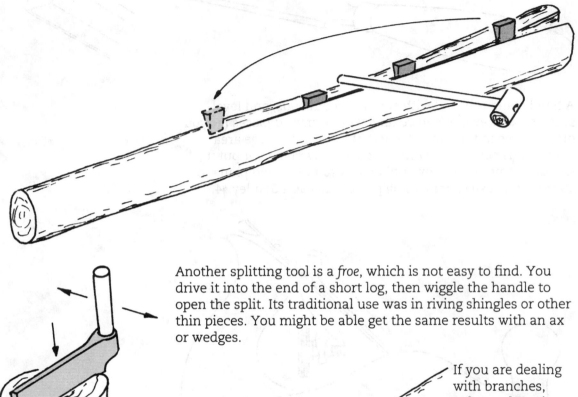

Another splitting tool is a *froe*, which is not easy to find. You drive it into the end of a short log, then wiggle the handle to open the split. Its traditional use was in riving shingles or other thin pieces. You might be able get the same results with an ax or wedges.

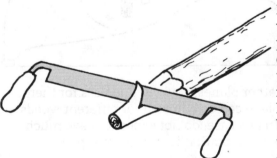

If you are dealing with branches, poles and rustic construction, a tool that will be useful is a *drawknife*. Its long blade is beveled on one side to make a cutting edge with the same section as a chisel. For most work, you pull it. With the bevel downwards and adjusting the angle of cut, you can regulate how much you remove. It will cut twigs from a pole, shave a point, or decorate angles by beveling. You might do the same with other tools, but the drawknife is quicker and more efficient.

Sharpening is done on an abrasive stone, lubricated either with thin oil or water—one or the other, as they do not mix. Precision woodworkers favor some exotic stones, but for your work it should be sufficient to have a manufactured stone of moderate grit. You might get a stone with different grits on opposite sides. The coarse grit wears away steel quickly, then you put on a sharper edge with the finer grit. Avoid a small stone: A 1"-x-2"-x-8" stone is ideal. Most tools are rubbed on the stone, but you can hold it in your hand like a file on an ax or drawknife.

You can usually see a blunt edge. Hold the tool with its edge up and look at it towards a light. A blunt edge will shine white.

Have the stone secure on a bench and lubricate it. Note the existing bevel on the chisel or plane blade. Hold it at this angle on the stone, with one hand controlling the tool and the fingers of the other hand applying pressure near the edge.

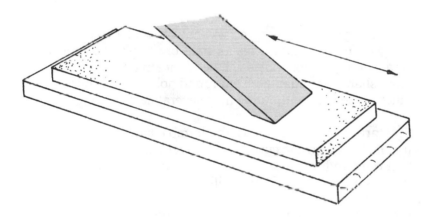

Stand with one foot in front of the other so you can swing your body to maintain the same angle on the stone as you move the tool over the whole surface. When you judge you have rubbed enough, wipe off the oil or water and feel toward the edge on the flat side. If there is roughness, that is a *wire edge* (shown exaggerated in the margin) indicating the bevel has been rubbed to sharpness and there is a particle of steel clinging along it.

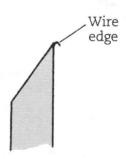

Wire edge

To loosen a wire edge, rub the flat side briefly on the stone, shown below to left. To remove it, slice across the edge of a piece of wood, shown below to right. If you are using a double stone, repeat the process on the fine surface enough to remove the marks left by the coarse grit. Keep the stone lubricated in use. If it rubs dry, it soon clogs and becomes ineffective.

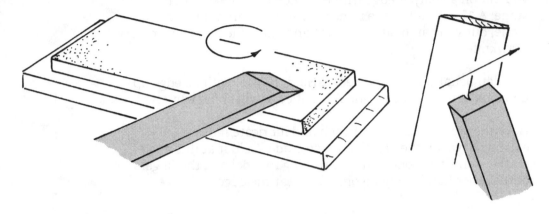

Drilling tools

Whatever you construct, you will need to make holes that will range from quite small ones for nails or screws to others of large diameter. Most holes will be round; in fact, even those of other shapes are adapted from round holes. You cannot do much woodwork without owning several hole-making tools.

For starting nails and screws the humble *bradawl* is the tool to use. Enter it with the cutting edge across the grain, then twist it backward and forward. This is also useful for accurately locating the centers of large drills.

It might seem primitive, but burning a hole can be satisfactory. Suppose you need a hole in an existing post and no other tools are available. Heat the end of a steel rod to redness, and push it through.

For holes within its capacity, a cordless electric drill is a valuable possession. If you have a drill with a cord, its uses are restricted to the near availability of a power point, unless you have a portable generator. A chuck capacity of ⅜ inch or ½ inch, besides drilling up to its size, will also take wood-boring bits of larger size, possibly up to 1 inch diameter in some woods.

Collect ordinary twist drills in plenty of small sizes. Although intended for metal, these are equally good in wood for screw holes and similar work, but the hole is rough. For smoother holes, you

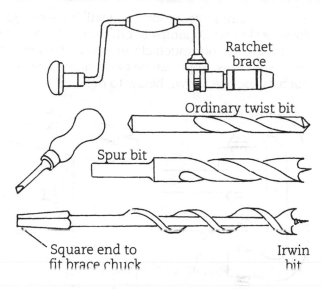

Ratchet brace

Ordinary twist bit

Spur bit

Square end to fit brace chuck

Irwin bit

will need spur bits. There are other wood-boring bits for power drills, but many of them are suitable only for shallow holes.

You will not get far before you discover a need to drill holes by hand. For this you will want a brace, preferably a ratchet one, which will allow you to work in restricted places. Bits have square ends to fit the brace chuck. Irwin bits are probably the best to use for deep holes because the screw point helps to draw the bit in.

A screwdriver bit to fit the brace will allow you to drive or withdraw large screws with much more leverage than any other way.

If you visit a tool store, you will probably find the array of tools offered both bewildering and tempting. Try to remember, though, that you can do nearly all your work with the basic tools already described. Delay obtaining others until you find a need for them.

Other tools

At some point in your work, you will have to squeeze parts together. A few C-clamps of different sizes are worth having (below to left), but much clamping can be done with improvisations. Rope can be twisted into a *Spanish windlass*, such as the one shown below to right.

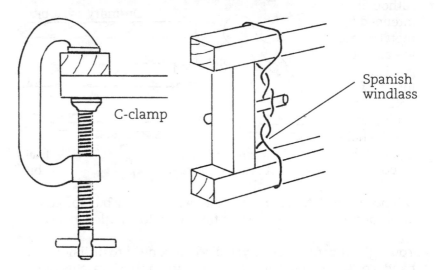

C-clamp

Spanish windlass

A wedge can put on considerable pressure, below to left. Better still are *folding wedges*, below to right, which put on a parallel thrust.

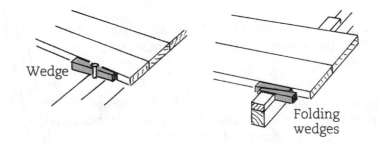

Wedge

Folding wedges

To tighten nuts and bolts, open-ended wrenches are best, but you also will need an adjustable wrench for odd sizes. You will find locking pliers are useful for many things besides tightening nuts.

It's helpful to have one or two files for trimming metal. You can use a coarse file on wood, but a better tool for quickly shaping a ragged wood end is a file-like *Surform* tool.

If you dig a hole for a post with a spade, you have to remove more soil than is necessary, then ram it back around the post. A post-hole borer is a good investment if you want to erect many posts because it does not remove more soil than necessary (below to left).

You can drive a post with a maul or sledgehammer, but a rammer is a tool that keeps the post upright as it is bounced to drive it in (below to right).

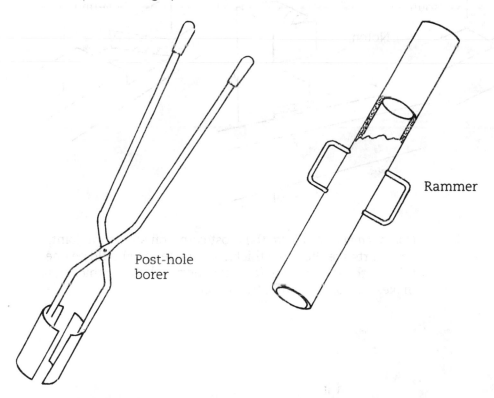

Rammer

Post-hole
borer

Much outdoor assembly of woodwork consists of putting a piece of wood on top of another and nailing or screwing it there, but in some situations it is better to cut joints.

Joints

If parts have to cross level, you will need a *halving joint* (shown below). You do not always need a full-depth joint. A shallow notch will provide a positive location and a resistance to slipping for a rail on a post. If a pull has to be resisted at a T-joint you can cut a halving joint in dovetail form.

Halving joints

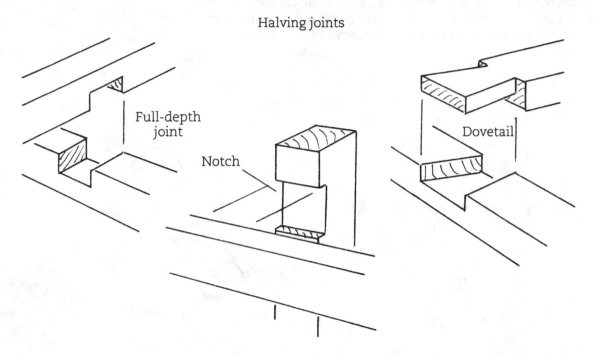

Full-depth joint

Notch

Dovetail

Mortises and tenons form the most common structural joint. If both parts are the same thickness, the tenon should be one-third of the thickness (left). If the mortised part is thicker, it makes a stronger joint if the tenon is thicker (right).

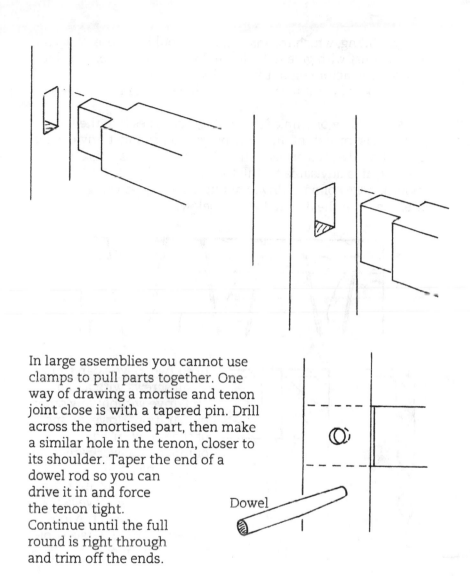

In large assemblies you cannot use clamps to pull parts together. One way of drawing a mortise and tenon joint close is with a tapered pin. Drill across the mortised part, then make a similar hole in the tenon, closer to its shoulder. Taper the end of a dowel rod so you can drive it in and force the tenon tight. Continue until the full round is right through and trim off the ends.

Dowel

Other joints and variations on these will be described where they occur in the "projects" section.

Fasteners

For most outdoor woodworking you will join parts with nails, screws, nuts and bolts, and glue.

You can find good, fully waterproof glues that are supplied in two parts and intended primarily for boat building. Some are not gap-filling, which means surfaces should fit close. You can mix sawdust with glue to fill limited spaces. However, no glue will be satisfactory on unseasoned wood. For outdoor woodwork, it is best to supplement glue with nails or screws.

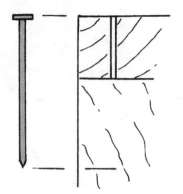

Nails should be of ample length. It is what goes into the lower part that is important. In many places you can just drive in, but in most hardwoods or near an end where there is a risk of splitting, it is advisable to drill the top part slightly undersize (at left). A row of nails driven at alternate angles will gain strength from the dovetail effect (below).

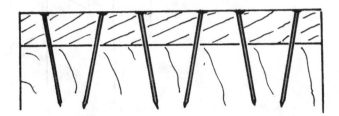

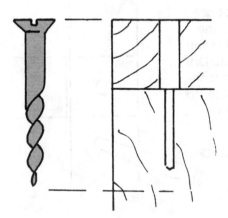

In softwood, you can start small screws with a hammer and drive without any other preparation. However, most of the screws used in outdoor woodwork are large and can be driven successfully only after proper drilling. Have a clearance hole in the top piece and an undersize hole in the bottom part .

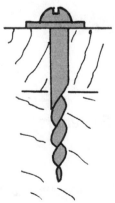

You can drill a short hole in softwood and let the screw pull in further, but you will need to drill the full depth in most hardwoods. How much you countersink the hole depends on the wood. The screw head will pull into softwood, but if you want the head to finish level in hardwood, you should at least partially countersink the hole. If you prefer roundhead screws, put a washer under the head.

Steel nails and screws should be galvanized or protected by some other sort of plating to reduce the risk of rust. Nails and screws in other metals are considerably more expensive. Rubbing a screw or nail with soap will make driving it easier.

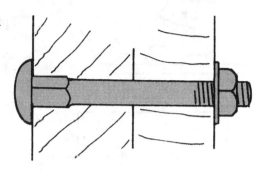

Bolts with nuts will pull parts together and secure them better than nails or screws, in many situations. Use large washers to prevent the head or nut from pulling into the wood. Carriage, or coach, bolts have the advantage of neat heads and square necks to pull into the wood and resist turning.

Not many parts will have to be riveted. You usually can make rivets from steel nails, but rivets made from the softer metals, such as copper and aluminum, are easier to use.

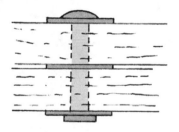

If you want to arrange parts to pivot against each other, as in folding chair legs, you can use a long rivet (probably cut from a thick nail) with large washers to prevent excessive wear on the wood. Use a ball peen hammer to spread the end of the rivet.

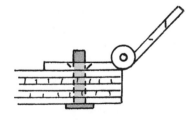

Most plywood you use will not be thick enough to offer much hold to screw threads, and this can become a problem when you want to fit hinges. Rivets are then better than screws. Use rivets or pieces of nail almost as thick as the diameter of the holes in the hinge. Cut them off to leave what you judge to be enough to spread and fill the countersink of the hinge holes. It should be sufficient for the rivet or nail heads to bear directly against the wood, but you could put washers under them.

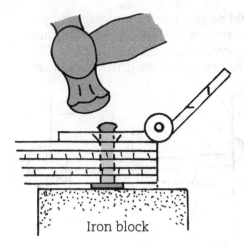

Support each rivet head on an iron block and hammer the rivet end to spread it into the countersunk hole, by working round the edges of it. A lot of moderate taps are better than a few heavy blows.

Iron block

Safety

USING WOODWORKING TOOLS need not be dangerous, if you are careful. Use edge tools away from you as far as possible. If you have two hands on the tool, you should not be able cut your hands. Be sure to have the wood secured before working on it, and remember that blunt tools require more force and, as a result, are potentially more dangerous than sharp ones.

Observe the manufacturer's instructions for power tools. See that electrical connections are properly made, and avoid improvised wiring. Disconnect power before opening or resetting a tool.

Wearing goggles is generally advisable—even in simple handwork, a splinter or metal chip could fly into your eye. Have a respirator or filter available for use in dusty conditions and make sure the filter is adequate for toxic fumes. With some power tools, it's a good idea to use earmuffs.

Avoid loose clothing, such as a hanging necktie or open sleeves. Some sort of coverall is the best protection. For much work you will want bare hands, but you might favor protective gloves for rough work and rubber or plastic gloves for messy or dangerous liquids.

Fences

Whatever your property, you will need fences of some sort. Fences might be necessary to define the limits of your land, to protect a garden from marauding animals, or to keep your own animals from wandering. On the other hand, you might want a fence that serves no functional purpose at all—one that simply decorates your property.

The most substantial fences are stone or brick walls. You could use metal uprights to support strands of barbed or electrified wire, supporting the wire with wood posts. You could add decorative, reinforced concrete panels. For the roughest fence to restrict animals you might stake spare pieces of corrugated iron, crates, box panels or anything else you have at hand.

However, most fences are constructed mainly or entirely from wood, and that is the material chosen for the examples in this chapter. Suitable woods are discussed on pages 1 through 9.

Some traditional fences have rails laid in a zigzag pattern (shown below), so the ends overlap without posts. Ideally, such fences will have posts; otherwise, these fences are not likely to remain intact for a long time. Unless you are trying to reproduce an early homestead, you probably won't want to construct this type of fence. But, if you do, be sure to have a large number of straight poles to use as rails, and drive large nails or spikes into the overlaps.

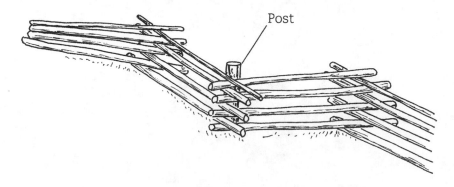

Post

Modern wood fences rely on posts to provide support. These are the key parts in fence-building. It does not matter how skillfully you make the rest of the fence; if posts become loose, wobble, rot, or collapse, it is difficult or impossible to restore the fence to sound and attractive condition.

A fence post must penetrate the ground sufficiently, so determine what kind of ground you have on your property. Clay provides better support than sandy soil. A fence that is to stand 4 feet to 5 feet above the ground will need posts sunk 2 feet to 3 feet, particularly if the fence is to withstand knocks by cattle or horses. As a rough guide, posts for field fences should have about one-third of their length in the ground.

A point on a post allows it to penetrate the ground easier as it is driven (shown at top right). However, this does not offer much resistance to the post's going deeper into the ground as time passes, so be warned that a fence over loose soil might sag. If you dig a hole in soft soil, it would be better to leave the bottom of the post square or to give it only a slight taper (shown at lower right). In extremely soft soil, you might put stones at the bottom of the hole.

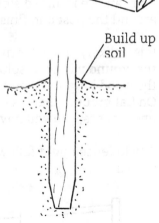
Build up soil

Whatever way you make the hole and drive the post, you should try to consolidate the soil around the driven post at least as compactly as it was before you started. A heavy piece of hardwood about 3 inches square makes a good rammer. It should not be possible to move the erected post any appreciable amount. After you have finished the fence, go back and ram the soil again. Avoid hollows, which would collect water around the posts. It would be better to build up soil.

Loads on a fence are nearly all sideways. If the soil is very loose and cannot be compacted enough, nail on a board to come just below the surface (at left) and increase the area of resistance in that direction.

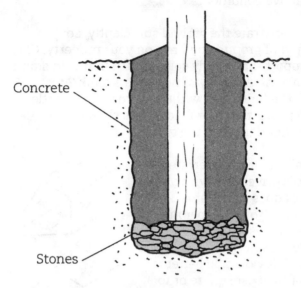

Concrete

Stones

Sinking posts directly into the ground should be adequate for most fences. You might need greater strength for a high fence or a gate post, though, and in that case, it is better to support the post with concrete. How you do this depends on circumstances, but a 4-inch post might go into 12-inch-square concrete about 24 inches deep. The hole does not have to be an exact square. You can use rammed stones at the bottom, then pour concrete around the post and finish it sloping at the top.

It is unlikely you will drive all posts the same amount or that the ground will be absolutely level, so it's a good idea to leave the wood long and trim the tops level after the posts are driven. On flat ground, there is no problem, but if there is a slope or unevenness, you will have to decide what to do.

A field fence might follow a general slope, such as the one shown.

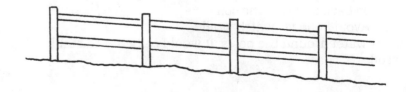

You can allow for slight undulations by having different-length posts, so rails will finish level.

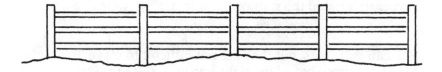

If possible, avoid sloping rails or infillings. They do not look right, particularly where they provide part of the general scene around a yard or garden. On a pronounced slope, you will have to arrange the fence in steps, as shown.

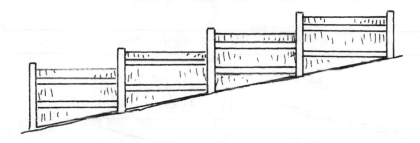

Never slope posts. They should be upright, whatever the lay of the land. A post that is not upright will be obvious immediately to any viewer, and it could affect the run of the fence. If you have a long spirit level that will measure plumb, that is the tool to use, but you can get the same result with a weighted string—*a plumb line.* Test each post in two directions at 90° to each other.

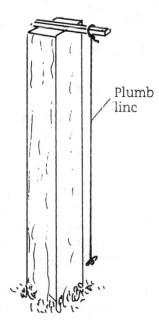

Plumb line

Spurs

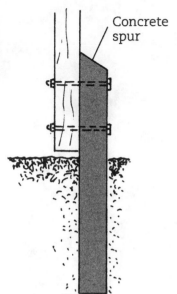

Concrete spur

Although most hardwoods and treated softwoods should have a long life directly in contact with soil, you could use concrete spurs to keep the wood above the ground (at left). You might ram earth around the spur or put it in a larger hole and pour concrete.

You can buy spurs, but they are not difficult to make. Put together a wood box of the right size with sides that can be knocked away (below). Grease iron rods of the same diameter as (or slightly larger than) the bolts you will be using, and fit the rods into holes in the bottom of the box. (It also helps to grease the wood surfaces that will be in contact with the concrete.)

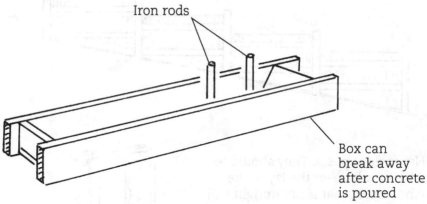

Iron rods

Box can break away after concrete is poured

Pour the concrete, and trowel it level. See that the rods remain upright. When the concrete has set, knock away the sides and drive out the rods.

Struts

In some situations, such as a high, closely boarded fence facing a strong prevailing wind, you might have to brace posts with struts, possibly only at intervals. If an end post is to take the strain of tensioned wire, you can provide a similar strut in the direction of the pull.

If a strut is to provide maximum strength to the fence, it needs something to thrust against. This means you have to dig down and position a thrust plate (shown below), which could be a board, a flat stone, or a piece of stiff sheet metal. Alternatively, pour concrete below and around the strut. In any case, ram soil tight after positioning the strut.

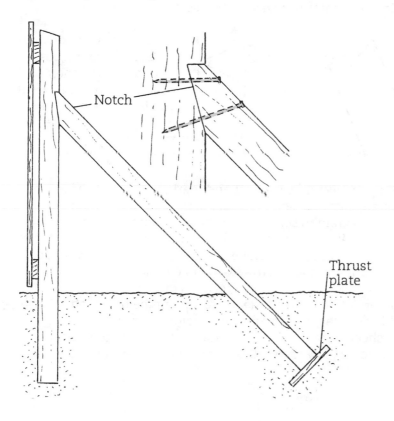

For greater strength, Notch the strut into the post. The notch need not be deep (¾ inch in a 4-inch post), but it is the fitted angle that provides resistance to the fence bending more than the nails do. The angle of the strut is not crucial—between 45° and 60° to the ground should be satisfactory.

Post tops

You need to consider the top of a post, both while it is being driven and when you finish it. Keep in mind that recently cut softwood posts are more likely to split than seasoned hardwood, so try to avoid splitting a post when you are driving it. Driving posts with a maul, particularly if its head is larger

Fences 43

than the size of the post, is less liable to start a split than the more concentrated hit of a sledgehammer. Another option is to spread the force of a hammer blow by holding a flat board on top of the post. (See the *Tools & techniques* section, pages 18 to 36, for more information about these tools.)

 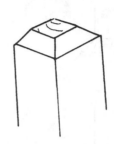

Whether you are driving a naturally round post or a square-sawn one, you can help avoid splitting if you bevel the post all around and keep the top reasonably square across rather than sloping.

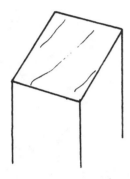

When you have driven a post and marked its top at the height required, cutting it square across is the simplest option, but that allows rain to settle and enter the grain, which could cause rot. Water is encouraged to run away if you cut the top at a slope. The steeper the slope, the better it will shed water, of course, but 45° is about the reasonable limit.

Another option is to cut the top to a point (below to left). You could add a separate overhanging pointed top (below center). Thin sheet metal turned down and nailed offers complete protection (below to right). Lead and zinc are suitable durable metals.

Post cut
to a point

Point added to
squared post top

Sheet metal

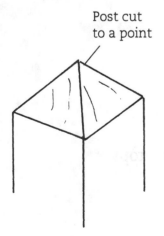 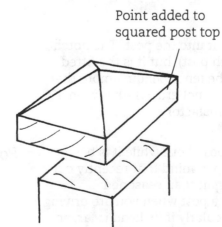 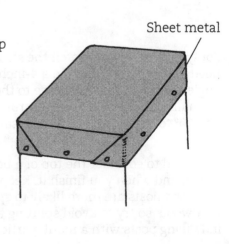

A basic fence might consist of posts 4 feet to 5 feet above the ground with two or more rails. Sections of wood for rails and spacing of posts depend on the strength required and the available wood. You could have rail joints at every post, but a nailed fence will be stronger if each rail extends over two bays. In other words, for posts spaced 7 feet apart, you will need 14-foot rails. Then joints can be on different posts at alternate levels.

For rails, you can use poles, either fully round or split, or you can use sawn wood. For a yard fence, you can use 2"-x-3" section if the posts are not too far apart, but for a field fence you will need 2"-x-6" (or larger). Lower rails do not always need to be as large section as the top ones.

Many fences will work best with three rails. If the rails will be at one side of the posts, arrange them toward the side on which the greater pressure can be expected (such as from animals).

On a nailed fence, bearing surfaces that meet should be flat. With sawn or planed wood, they will be flat already. However, with round or split rails, you might have to actually cut flats (shown to the right).

Butt the ends closely on a post (below to left). You get nails into different grain lines on a post, and you can reduce the risk of splitting if you cut meeting rail ends at an angle (below to right).

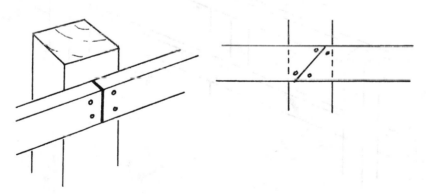

Notching a post increases strength in the joint (shown below at left) and prevents later movement. If the fence will be boarded and you want the posts level with the rails and boards, you'll probably want to notch both parts (shown below at right).

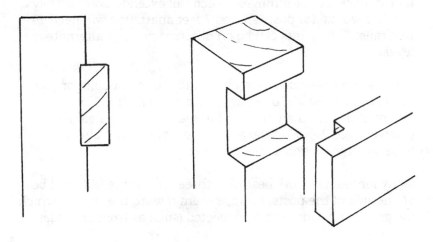

For horizontal loads expected to be the same from opposite sides, you could arrange posts at alternate sides.

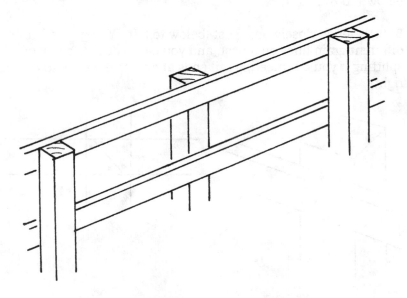

You could drive posts in pairs, so the rails are between, or you could arrange rails alternately on opposite sides. Either way, put bolts through the whole assembly.

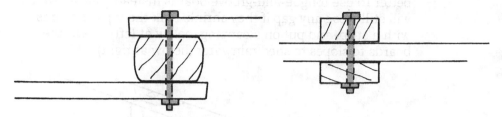

Rails could go through mortises in the posts. These are difficult to cut when the post is in position, so you would have to make the mortise in advance and sink the posts so rail positions are level.

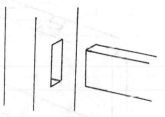

Cut sawn rail ends at acute angles to overlap (below at left) Taper round or split pole ends the other way (below at right). If you cut the mortises deeper than necessary and have the rails' ends at long angles, it should be possible to move some rails sufficiently to remove or replace them, yet leave them secure at other times. This allows you to make a temporary gap in the fence when needed.

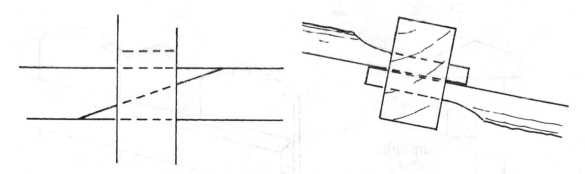

Rails between posts might be all you need to restrain stock or to mark a boundary, but if you want to provide privacy, form a windbreak, or add decoration, the fence has to be made more solid, usually by attaching vertical boards to the rails.

Infilling

If privacy is important, you probably do not want to use plain vertical boards since they will expand and contract, leaving gaps. You could cover them with narrow strips, but it would be better to use tongue-and-groove boards instead (below), which will still close any gap if they shrink. Link the tops of boards with a strip, and put on a capping (below at left), or cut the boards to slopes to shed rainwater (below at right).

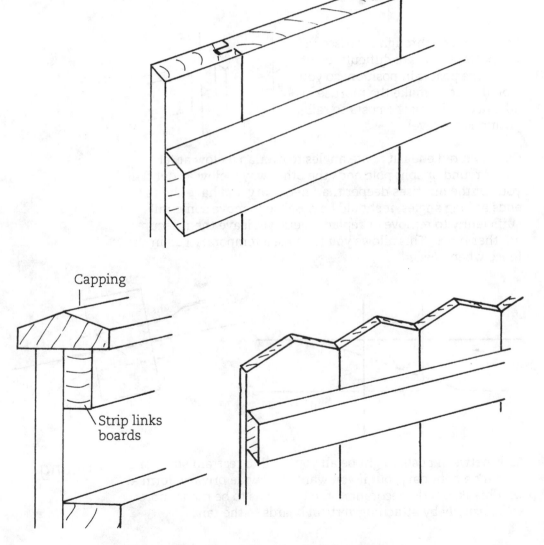

Capping

Strip links boards

Solid boarding could put the fence under considerable strain in a strong wind. If you put the boards alternately on opposite sides of the rails with slight overlaps, as shown (below), wind resistance is much less and there is still reasonable privacy. The fence also breaks up the flow of the wind and acts as a snow guard, if the object of the fence is to protect plants or delicate crops.

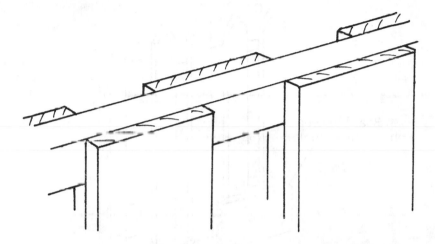

You can buy prepared decorative panels intended as infill for fencing. Their standard size will set the spacing and height of posts, so buy them before you start work. Decorative infill panels are made with square corners, so they can be fitted with no trouble over flat ground. If you are working on a slope, however, they should be stepped; on uneven ground, they should be set to the highest position. In both cases you will have to arrange other boarding below all or some of the panels.

Picket fences

A lower fence around a yard or garden usually employs *pickets* or *palings,* which are vertical pieces of wood nailed to rails with varying amounts of decoration. Besides being there to provide a pleasing appearance, a picket fence stops dogs and all but the smallest animals, while allowing flowers and climbing plants to develop.

A rustic fence with split pole rails and split pieces that are little more than saplings is functional and looks right in a suitable

setting (far left). However, most picket fences are made with prepared wood. For a picket fence at waist height, you could use 1-inch-by-3-inch wood with 1- to 2-inch spaces. Use a piece of scrap wood of the chosen width to get the gaps and bottoms even (below). Keep the bottoms of pickets clear of the ground. If you choose, you can cover the pickets with a board to keep out small animals.

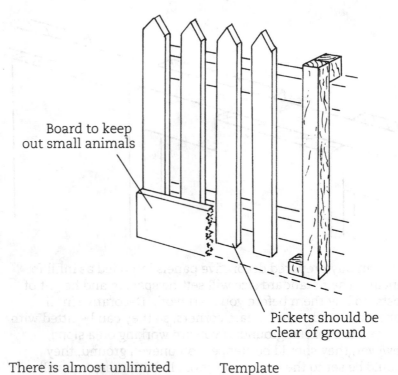

Board to keep out small animals

Pickets should be clear of ground

There is almost unlimited scope for decorating picket fences, particularly at the tops of pieces, which need not be the same width or arranged in a straight line. To ensure uniformity of shape, prepare all pickets in advance. Even if the decoration is just a single or double slope, variations along a fence will appear obvious.
Set guides on a table saw or use a simple template.

Template

Possible patterns for the tops of pickets are almost limitless, but a few are suggested here. Single slopes or symmetrical designs can be arranged alternate ways (right). Semicircular edge shapes can be made by clamping pickets together and drilling through the meeting edges (below).

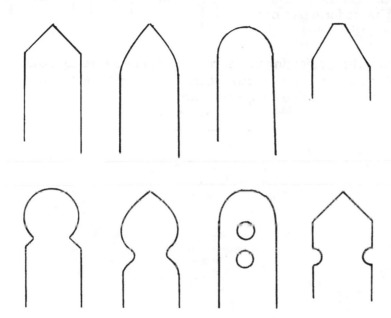

It is the general effect that matters. With just a few pickets, individual elaborate tops might be worth having, but with a row of 50 or so, the eye follows the whole scene, and details are less important. Your labor will be less in mass-producing something simple.

You can further decorate the fence by varying the line of the tops of pickets. You can stagger the heights, as shown, or the lower pickets could be narrower than the high ones.

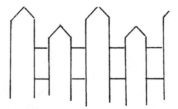

Another option is for the tops to follow a curve downward or upward. You could keep the posts low so they are hidden by pickets, or take them higher to form part of the decoration.

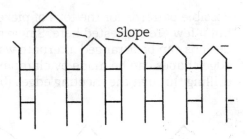

Somewhere adjoining the fence there will be a gate. Consider this as part of the decorative scheme. It could have its own pickets to continue the general pattern.

Gates

IN A FEW SITUATIONS, YOU CAN LEAVE A GAP in a fence or arrange a temporary barrier, but in most cases you will want to close it with a gate or door. If you want people, but not animals, to pass, you might build a stile. Gates and doors can be a source of trouble due to poor design, construction, or materials. Even if the gate is sound, it might sag due to movement in an insecure gatepost. Building a satisfactory gate or door need not be difficult.

Design

If a gate is solid, as it would be if consisting of a single piece of plywood with framing, it cannot get out of shape. Most gates are built of parts, so movement between the parts, if it is not restricted, will cause the gate to sag. The gate gets all its external support at one side only; as a result, the whole weight comes on the hinges between the edge of the gate and its post. Even if you make a door apparently solid with many vertical boards, the boards will slide against each other if they are not suitably braced. The door edge might touch the ground or the latch will no longer connect.

To prevent sagging, you have to build triangular frameworks into the gate or door. A single hinged barrier (at right) cannot sag unless the diagonal strut is so weak that it bends or breaks under compression. A triangle cannot be pushed out of shape.

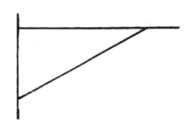

The barrier framework can be extended into a gate. The diagonal is still in compression, but you also have a choice of having the diagonal go either way. Loads now try to stretch the diagonal piece, so it is in tension.

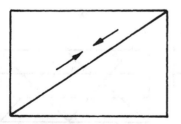 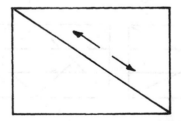

Providing ends are secured to resist movement, a piece of wood in tension need not be quite as large a section as one in compression, but in practice you would probably make them the same. The next step is to share the load with diagonals in both directions.

Hinge side

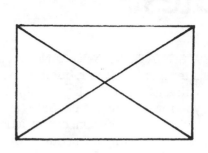

The more parts that are connected to the diagonal piece, the greater will be the resistance to sagging. On a gate you could bolt to every rail crossing. With palings there should be ample nails through the diagonal to every one (below).

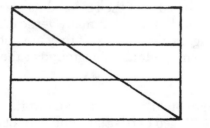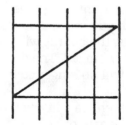

A strut or brace at a very flat angle is not as effective as one nearer upright—45 degrees is a reasonable angle. Suppose a gate is twice as wide as it is high: Then braces across would be at rather flat angles (below far left). It would be better to divide the width into two (below center). Taking the brace higher on the hinged side (below far right) increases strength as well as adding interest to the appearance.

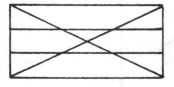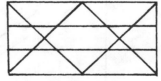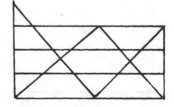

If a door or gate is to pass people, the clear opening should not be less than 30 inches, unless there are space restrictions that cannot be avoided, and 36 inches might be better, particularly if you expect to carry loads through. A single gate can be made to close an opening to pass cattle or a vehicle, but for a wide opening you should consider double gates. They could be the same width or different if you know there will be times when opening a narrow one only will pass people or a few animals. Besides being able to link the gates where they meet, you will need a bolt or other attachment to the ground, strong enough to resist animals thrusting from either side. A single gate is less vulnerable to animal pressure.

When a fence consists of palings, a small gate that forms a break in its line can be made with matching palings. Such a small wicket gate need not be of heavy construction, but it should be properly braced to hold its shape.

Wicket gate

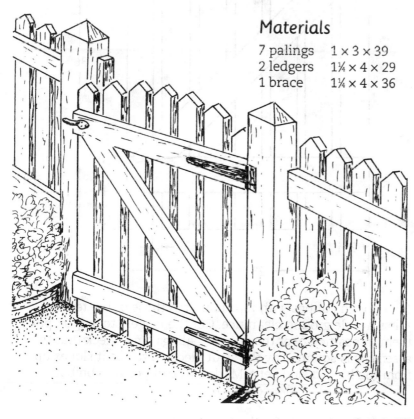

Materials

7 palings	1 × 3 × 39
2 ledgers	1¼ × 4 × 29
1 brace	1¼ × 4 × 36

Posts should be secure, particularly on the hinge side, and they can be of larger section than those along the fence. Be careful to set them plumb. A gate made even slightly out of shape to suit an inaccurate opening will look wrong.

Palings should match those on the fence. Gate rails, called *ledgers,* could come in line with the fence rails, but may be smaller section. Sizes indicated in the illustration will have to be adapted to suit your needs.

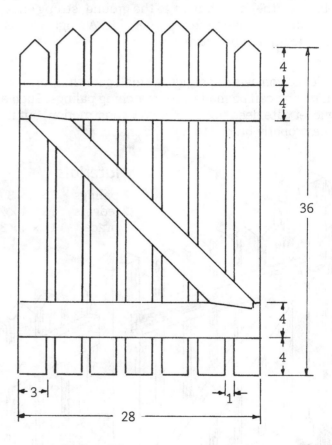

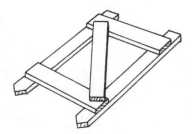

Cut enough palings with tops to match those of the fence. Allow ample ground clearance. Cut the ledgers to length, put them in position over the outside palings, and check that the assembly is square. Lay the strut piece on top so it slopes up from the hinged side (left). Mark the strut position on both ledgers and the ledger positions on the strut. With these marks as guides cut the notches in the ledgers (right). Notches can be ½ inch deep.

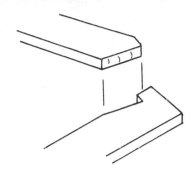

Nail the outer palings to the ledgers. Check overall squareness and that the gate fits its opening. Cut the end of the strut to fit its notch. Next, check the other end, and cut that to make a tight fit. Space and nail on the other palings to the ledgers and the strut. For extra strength, use waterproof glue in all joints.

Hang the gate with T-hinges. Put a stop strip on the opposite post, and arrange a catch or fastener at the top ledger level. Allow ample clearance at the sides of the gate. The hinged side could be ¼ inch from the post when closed, with up to ½ inch at the other side.

Boarded door

If you have a high, closed fence, any door in or adjoining it also should be high if privacy or protection from the wind is to be maintained. You have to make a closely boarded door of about the same height as the fence. If this is about 6 feet, the doorposts have to be at least that height, which could lead to problems if they become even slightly insecure. Although the posts should be firmly set in the ground and probably of larger section than those farther along the fence, you can brace them with a rail across the top. If this is about 7 feet from the ground, it will not impede anyone passing underneath. A straight bar is shown, but you could use this place above the door for decoration such as name or number.

Materials

4 boards   1 × 8½ × 74
3 ledgers   1¼ × 5 × 34
2 braces   1¼ × 5 × 42

The sizes suggested (below) will serve as a guide to suitable materials when you design your own door. A tall door should be made with three ledgers to hold the boards flat and provide positions for three hinges. Two diagonal braces fit between them sloping up from the hinged side.

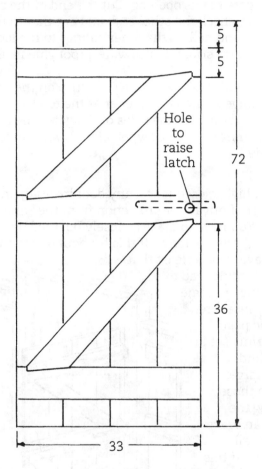

Hole to raise latch

5

5

72

36

33

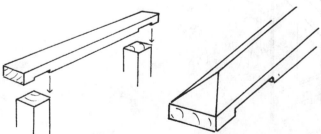

Arrange the gateposts upright and parallel, then fit the rail across the top, as shown far left. Notches lock the posts at the correct width. You could leave this as a parallel piece of wood, or, if you have a similar capping on the adjoining fence, you could shape the top to shed water (left).

Prepare boards to make the door about ¾ inch less than the space between the posts. Allow ground clearance and level the top with the fence. You could use plain or tongue-and-groove boards. The boards do not have to be the all same width, but at least put wider boards on the outside for strength.

Make ledgers and braces in a similar way to those described for the wicket gate as shown on pages 56 and 57. The gate looks best if the middle ledger is above half the door height. Although you could nail the parts, it would be better to use screws throughout or in addition to nails. Take sharpness off all exposed ends and edges. Hang the gate with T-hinges, and arrange a stop strip on the other gatepost.

The gate's fastener should be one that can be operated from both sides. You can buy a latch or lock with handles on both sides, or you can make a simple latch yourself out of hardwood The latch should be fairly long. The pivot screw could be almost to the center of the ledger; a large, roundhead screw with a washer each side of the latch would be suitable. When you have tested the action of the latch, put projecting screws above and below it to limit its movement. Make the catch block substantial.

Toggle handle

Catch block

There are at least two ways to operate the latch from the opposite side. Drill a large hole so you can put a finger or stick through to lift the latch, or use a cord, taken through the hole to a toggle handle. You can even provide both methods, if you wish.

If you have a number of natural poles up to 4 inches diameter, you might want to make a gate from them, particularly if the adjoining fence is also made from whole or split poles. Two

Rustic gates

versions are possible. For a gate up to about 4 feet square you could use poles 2-inch to 3-inch round for rails, with 3-inch to 4-inch round for uprights.

Materials for Gate #1

1 upright	6 feet × 3- to 4-inch diameter
1 upright	4 feet × 3- to 4-inch diameter
5 rails	5 feet × 2- to 3-inch diameter
1 pivot block	2 × 4 × 8
1 top pivot block	1½ × 4 × 15
1 latch	1 × 2 × 18

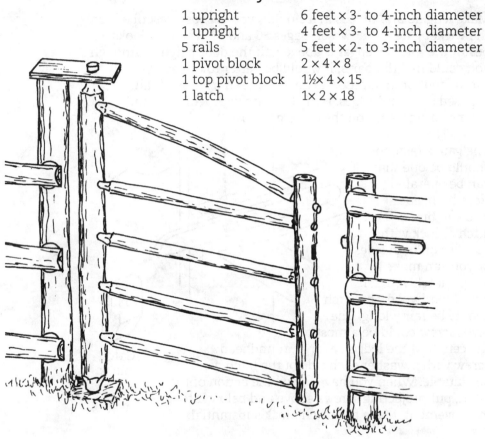

Except for the sloping top rail, the gate is not strutted to resist sagging and for this it depends on rigidity in the joints. If the gate is to be larger or if you want to use wood of greater diameter, you could split 4-inch or 5-inch poles for rails and brace, then use round pieces for the uprights.

Materials for Gate #2

1 upright	6 feet × 4- to 5-inch diameter
1 upright	4 feet × 4- to 5-inch diameter
4 rails	5 feet × 4- to 5-inch half-round
1 brace	7 feet × 4- to 5-inch half-round
1 pivot block	2 × 4 × 8
1 top pivot block	1½ × 4 × 15
1 latch	1 × 2 × 18

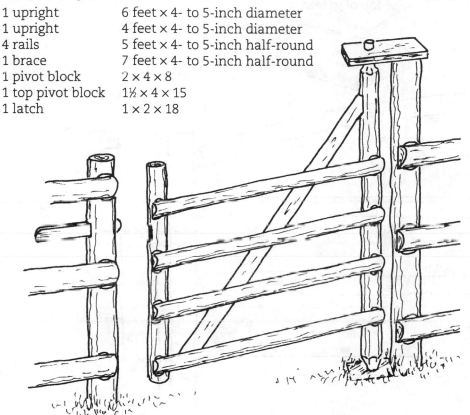

Gate #1

Prepare the hinged side first. The pivots should be 2-inch-diameter, if possible (for some hardwoods, though, you could make them 1½-inch-diameter). Make a block to sink in the ground, with a hole for the pivot (shown on next page). Make a piece to fit on top of the gatepost with a matching hole, and taper the ends of the pole that will make that side of the gate so the pole will turn in the holes. The pole might turn stiffly at first, but it will soon become easier as the gate is used.

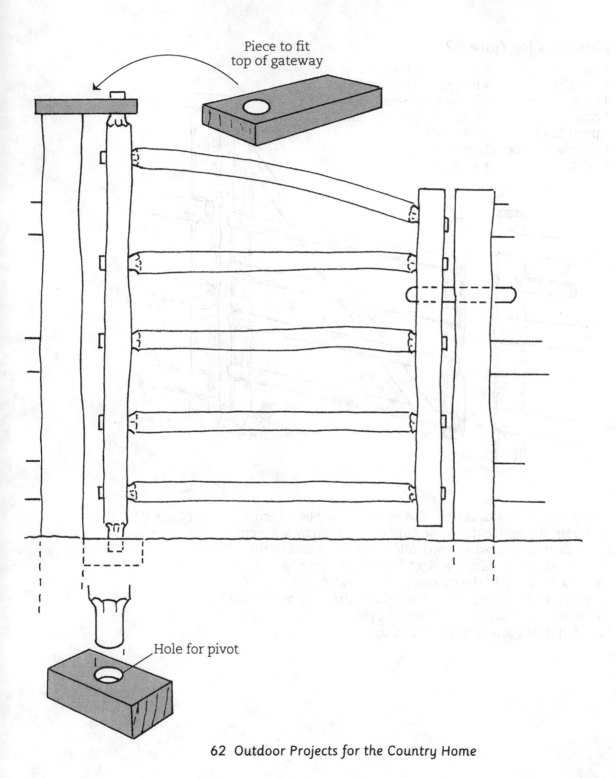

Piece to fit
top of gateway

Hole for pivot

For this gate with round rails, mark this and the other upright for rail holes to suit the chosen size of rails. The holes should be 1½ inches or larger for strength in the joints. At the top, you can allow for a straight or curved sloping rail.

The rails should be made to drive in and extend a little. Before final assembly, put saw cuts across the rail ends so you can drive in wedges, shown in margin. Keep in mind that unseasoned wood can be expected to shrink and tighten the joints.

Next, check squareness. By varying the penetration of rail ends you can make adjustments. Because the gate starts slightly high at the opening side, the effects of initial sagging should be insubstantial.

You can use any sort of catch, but a wood slide is appropriate to this gate. Cut a slot in the gatepost for a parallel piece of wood to slide easily. Cut a matching slot in the gate upright, but make it an easy fit. Cut deeper to allow for the gate sagging a little.

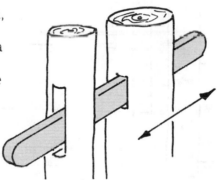

For the gate with split rails (see page 61), make the pivot upright with ends the same as for the first gate, but cut flats instead of holes at the rail positions.

Gate #2

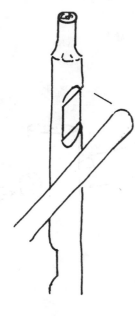

You can arrange a top rail in the same manner as the first gate, or, to ensure rigidity, you can make it as a brace crossing the other rails.

Let the rails into the uprights with flats cut at no more than one-fourth the thickness. Arrange the brace to bolt to each rail and at the top let it into a notch on the opposite side to the rails (below).

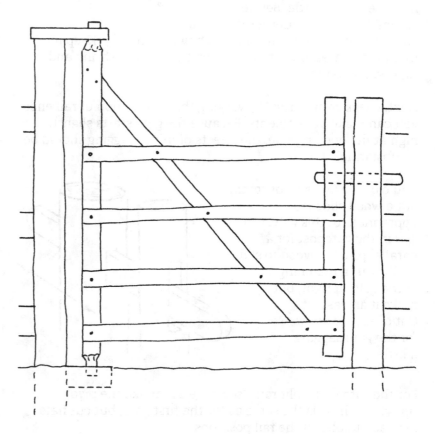

You could use long screws for joining rails to the uprights, but bolts through would be better.

An alternative to screws or bolts would be to drill through for hardwood pegs ¾-inch or 1-inch-diameter.

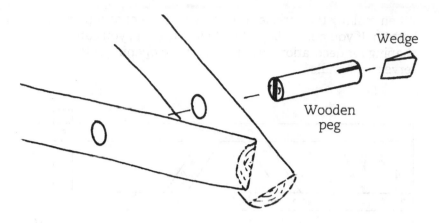

Wedge

Wooden
peg

You can hold the pegs with waterproof glue, drive wedges into saw cuts, or use wedges as well as glue. Arrange the saw cuts across the grain of the rail on that side, so that a driven wedge expands the end of the peg in the direction of the rail grain. You could cut the ends of the wedged pegs level with the rail surfaces, but it's fine to let them project in this type of gate. Finish the gate with a latch similar to that on the first gate.

You can make a gate of simple construction entirely from 2-inch-by-4-inch softwood or hardwood, all joined with ½-inch carriage bolts. Any reasonable size is possible, but a gate 7 feet wide by 4 feet high is described as an example (below). It could be used as a field or yard gate.

Bolted gate

Materials

2 uprights	2 × 4 × 56
4 rails	2 × 4 × 86
2 braces	2 × 4 × 65

When making the gate, let the uprights project at top and bottom. If you allow about 4 inches at the top, you can do some shaping for decoration and the top at the opening side can serve as a handle.

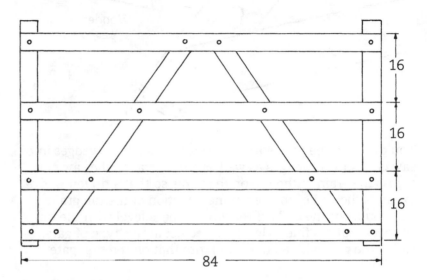

Make the two uprights identical, and mark the positions of rails. Cut the four rails to length. Drill centrally at each crossing for the bolts, which are best made a drive fit in the holes.

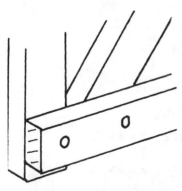

Assemble these parts temporarily flat on the ground, with the rails underneath. Check squareness by comparing diagonal measurements. Lay the diagonal brace pieces in place, and mark their positions on the rails. Mark and drill bolt holes. The braces meet on the top rail and go close into the bottom corners (at left).

Trim ends to length, do any shaping, and take sharpness off edges. If the wood is not already treated with preservative, treat the wood before assembly. If you are using a painted finish, paint meeting parts before bolting them together. Have the carriage bolt heads all on one side, and use washers under the nuts at the other side.

You could hang the gate with large T-hinges over the top and bottom rails. However, if the gate is very heavy, it would be better to use the type of hinge that fits on a pin on the gatepost (at right). Bolt these hinges through top and bottom rails.

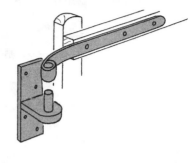

A simple catch to use is one is made from a strip of steel about ¼-inch-by-1-inch section, arranged as a loop to pivot on a bolt through the top of the gatepost. Put a block or strip on the post to prevent the gate being pushed the wrong way.

There is always a risk that a gate might be left open so animals can stray. If you and your family are the only ones to use a gate, you will see that it is shut after you, but if the gate is on a path where many people have access, the risk of an ordinary gate being left open is much greater. In that case you can make an enclosed wicket gate, which will pass one person at a time, but is always closed to animals.

The gate swings between two posts that form stops. A V-shaped barrier allows a person who has pushed the gate halfway to get around its end to the other side.

Enclosed wicket gate

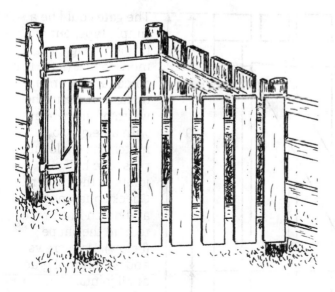

Materials

4 posts	5 inches diameter, 48 inches tall
4 barrier rails	2 × 4 × 60
14 barrier palings	1½ × 5 × 46
2 gate rails	1½ × 4 × 29
2 gate uprights	1½ × 4 × 30
1 gate brace	1½ × 4 × 32
5 gate palings	1½ × 5 × 42

In the example, it is assumed the gate will be located in a fence with round posts and flat or half-round rails, but you can adapt the design to suit other fences. The gate and its assembled barrier are described with pickets, but you could build a stop to animals in other ways.

Set out the ground plan as shown on opposite page. The gate is 27 inches wide and is shown swinging through 90°. The precise angle is not important, but something near that gives a satisfactory action. The space within the enclosure allows a gap sufficient for a person to pass when the gate is at half its swing.

Posts can be about 5 inches diameter. At three of them the rails are notched in the usual way. At the point of the V enclosure, however, the fence rails are notched at a level to suit the line of the fence, then the enclosure rails are positioned to miss them. Let the enclosed barrier rails into the posts about half their thickness. Pickets could be any suitable wood, but the suggested sizes are 5 inches wide with 2-inch gaps.

If the gate is in a field fence, there would be no need to decorate the tops of the pickets, but if it is near your house or part of a yard fence, you can decorate the pickets in any of the ways described earlier.

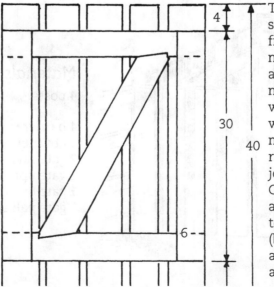

The gate could be a simple type, but a framed design is more robust (left). For a neat appearance, make a frame to the width of the gate and with a height to match the enclosure rails. Use halving joints at the corners. Check squareness and notch in a brace to hold the shape (below). Use screws and waterproof glue at all joints.

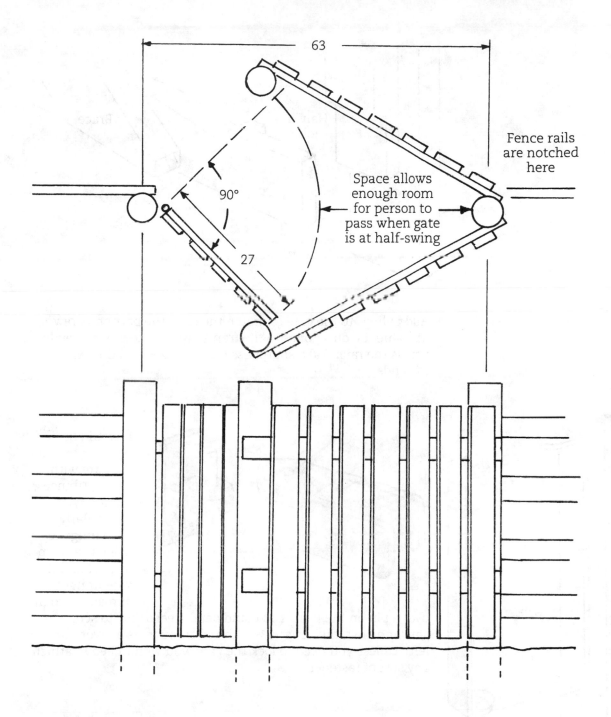

63

90°

27

Fence rails
are notched
here

Space allows
enough room
for person to
pass when gate
is at half-swing

Gates 69

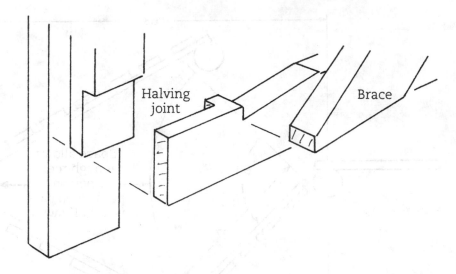

Halving joint

Brace

Add palings to the gate to match those on the barrier. Screw and glue the outer ones to the frame, and space others evenly across the rails. Take sharpness off the edges and the exposed top ends.

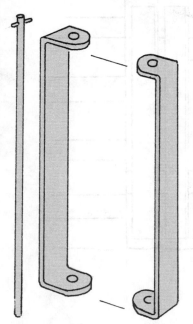

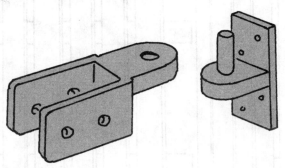

It would be possible to hang the gate with strong T-hinges, but a particularly good hinge to use has a strap to go round the gate upright and a hole to fit over a pin on the post. You could bend steel strips to screw to gate and post, then pass a ½-inch rod through as a pivot (far left). Unless you need to lock the gate, you won't need to attach any sort of fastener.

The traditional field gate has five bars, with spaces closer towards the bottom to hold back smaller animals and with ample bracing to prevent sagging. The width can be arranged to suit your needs, but the example is 11 feet wide. The sections of wood could be used for a narrower gate or for one up to 2 feet wider.

Construction should be with straight-grained hardwood, preferably planed to the sizes in the materials list, although a sawn finish might be acceptable in some circumstances. The top rail is shown tapered from 5 inches deep at the hinged side (where greater strength is needed) to 3 inches at the free side (for lightness). If you are unable to arrange the taper, you could use a parallel piece 4 inches deep. Rails are attached to the uprights with mortise-and-tenon joints. The braces tenon into the top rail but are held at each other rail with a ½-inch bolt.

Materials

1 upright	4 × 5 × 56
1 upright	3 × 3 × 56
1 top rail	3 × 5 × 132
4 rails	⅞ × 4 × 132
4 braces	¾ × 3 × 80

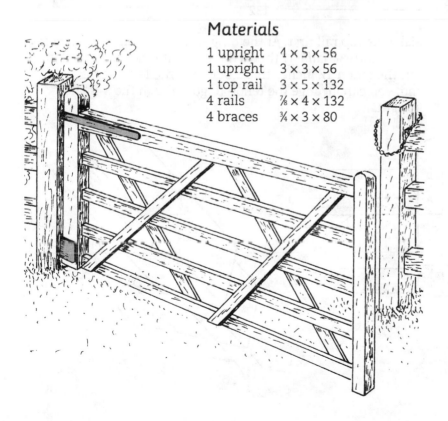

Prepare the two uprights. Round the tops and mark on the positions of the rails (below). You can alter the overall height or the rail spacing at this stage to suit stock, but the drawing sizes should suit most animals.

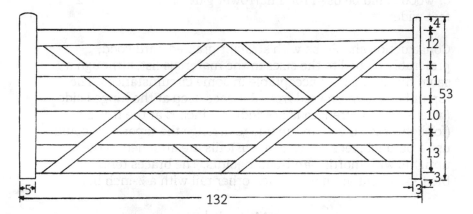

Make the top rail first. At the hinge end allow for a tenon going into a mortise halfway through the upright (below to the left). Cut the tenon 1¾ inches thick (below to the left). At the free end, you can arrange the tenon to go through the 3-inch upright.

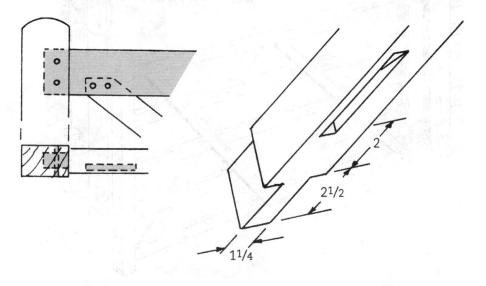

The four lower rails are the same. Do not reduce their ends for tenons, but take them their full thickness into the uprights, halfway on the hinged post and through the free post.

Make a dry assembly with the uprights and the top and bottom rails on a level surface, either on the ground or on trestles. Check squareness by comparing diagonal measurements. You can expect a slight initial sagging when the gate is first put into use. To allow for this, make the gate slope up from the hinge side just a degree or so more than 90° when you mark out for the braces and do the first assembly.

Lay the diagonal braces in position and mark on the top and bottom rails where joints will come. Although the braces will be on opposite sides, you can do this initial marking on the side that is uppermost, and then transfer over later.

Mark the ends of the rails for joints. At the top, each brace will be tenoned into the top rail 2 inches from the upright and tenoned in a similar way at opposite sides at the center. At their bottoms, mark where the braces overlap the bottom rail.

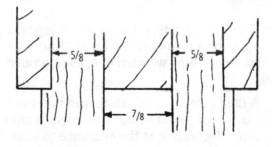

When you are satisfied you have marked the positions correctly, take the pieces apart and cut the mortise-and-tenon joints. Use the actual wood as a guide to sizes, but if

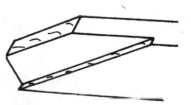

you have made it as specified, you have to leave ⅞ inch for the rails so that the braces come each side of it with ⅝-inch-thick tenons. Cut the pointed ends off square (right), and allow for the mortises being off-center to suit the braces each side of the rails.

Secure all joints with waterproof glue, and wedge the rail ends at the small post outside. Each of these, and the joints at the hinged end, should also have two ½-inch hardwood pegs through. The joints in the top rail are best arranged for draw-boring: As tapered pegs are driven through, they pull the tenons tight into the mortises, at ends and braces.

Assemble with the gate supported on trestles on a flat surface. Sight across to see that you do not make up the parts with a twist. Check squareness as you proceed. Make all pegged and glued joints first. Drill for bolts where the braces cross the bottom rail and fit the bolts with washers each side, using glue, as well, if desired. Drill and bolt at the crossings of other rails. Allow time for glue to set before moving the assembly.

The gate is heavy and requires a strong post on the hinged side, probably 6-inch square or round hardwood, held firm with a concrete base. Although the other post will not have to take so much load, it will look best if it is made to match. If the gate is required to swing only one way, it can overlap and be stopped by that post.

Most load will come on the top hinge, which could be the type with a strap each side of the top rail and bolts through. This can pivot on a substantial pin on the post. The bottom hinge could be similar, although you might be able to fit a type with a screw adjustment that would allow you to correct the swing of the gate.

At the other side, if the gate overlaps the post, the fastener could be a chain and padlock. Otherwise, fit a bought latch or make a sliding wooden one, as described for other gates.

Ornamental gates

A field gate has a job to do and has a certain beauty in its fitness for purpose, but you might want to make something more decorative at the entrance to your drive or some other featured access to your property. The gates here are basically the same as a field gate, but you can get the ornamental effect by extending the upright and brace on the hinged side upward and by shaping the top of all uprights.

You might choose to make a single gate, but two gates are sometimes more suitable. A matching pair is attractive, but there is often an advantage in having one gate narrower than the other; then if you want to walk through you open only the narrow gate. For a vehicle or animals you open the wider gate or both. For the sake of a balanced appearance, it is worthwhile having one gate twice as wide as the other. Then the diagonal braces can be arranged to give a near-symmetrical pattern.

The gates shown below and on next page are assumed to have an overall width of 12 feet, but you could use the design for an opening of any other width by making the narrow gate one-third of the total width.

Materials

2 uprights	4 × 4 × 71
2 uprights	3 × 3 × 60
1 rail	3 × 3 × 96
1 rail	3 × 3 × 48
3 rails	1 × 3 × 96
3 rails	1 × 3 × 48
2 braces	1 × 3 × 80
4 braces	1 × 3 × 60

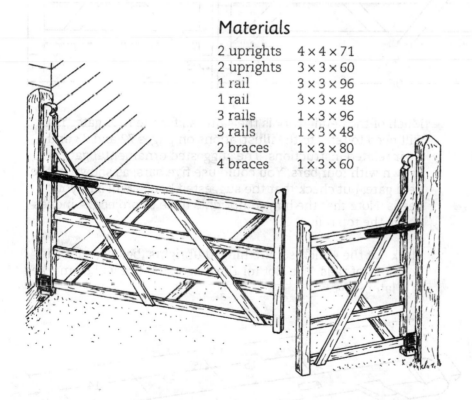

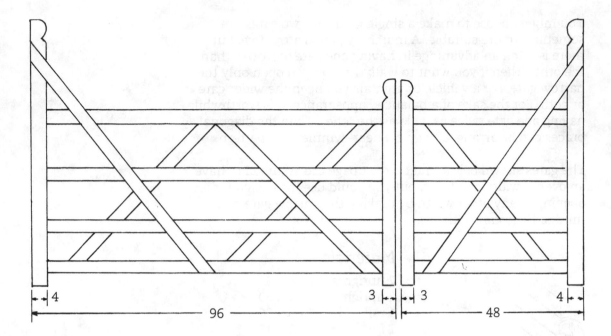

Much of the detail work is the same as for the field gate. You will need to refer to the illustrations on pages 72 and 73 and their related instructions. The suggested ornamental gate is shown with four bars. You could use five bars, as shown in the field gate, but check that the suggested height will suit your needs. Note that the hinged uprights have to project 24 inches above the top rail.

Mark out the 4-inch-square hinged uprights (below), with the positions of rails. The slot for the diagonal brace will be marked at a later stage.

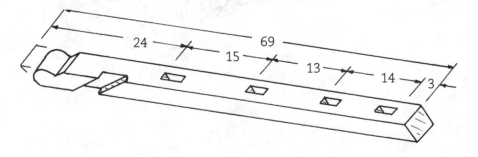

Mark the 3-inch-square uprights (right) with matching rail positions and a shorter top.

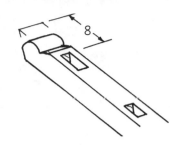

The shaped tops should be uniform; variations will spoil the appearance of the gates. Make a hardboard or card template such as the one shown below for marking the shape. On the 4-inch width, the shape is extended straight back.

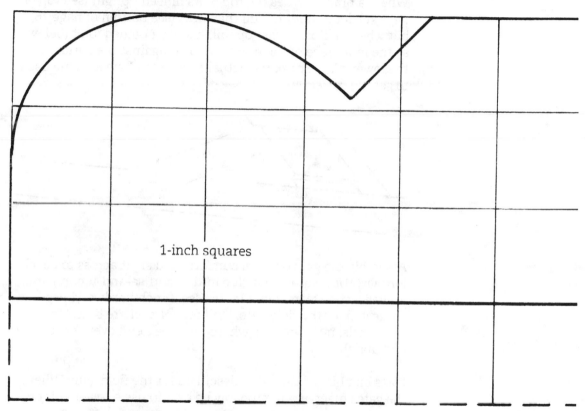

1-inch squares

Make the top rails to tenon into the 4-inch uprights and to go through the 3-inch ones. The three lower rails go into the uprights the same amount, but they are not reduced in thickness. Work on both gates at the same time so the parts will match.

Make a dry assembly of the gates with top and bottom rails attached to the uprights, truing and checking in the same way as for the field gate. Put the diagonal braces across, all on one side for marking. Mark their positions on every piece they cross and mark on them the positions of joints. In the top rail, allow for mortises 2 inches from the joints (see page 72) at the 3-inch upright and at the center of the top rail of the wide gate (see page 73). Cut tenons on the braces to suit the mortises (see page 73).

Where a brace crosses the top of its hinged upright (see top of page 76), let it in for its full thickness (see bottom of page 76) but where it crosses the top rail, make a notched joint (below). so the inner face of the brace will bear against the surfaces of the lower rails. Check the actual thickness of wood being used to get the correct fit.

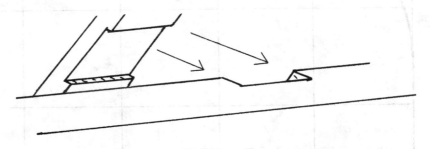

Assemble the gate on level supports and sight across to check for twist. Use waterproof glue in the mortise-and-tenon joints as well as between bolted faces. Use ½-inch hardwood pegs, as suggested for the field gate. Drill for bolts where braces cross lower rails; put two bolts where braces extend over the top rail and upright.

Posts and hinges can be as described for the field gate. Where the gates meet, it will probably be best to use a tower bolt on the wide gate to fit into a socket in the ground (left), then you need a latch on the narrow gate to hold it to the wide one at a height that can be reached through or by leaning over from the other side. Another option is to make your own hardwood latch (right).

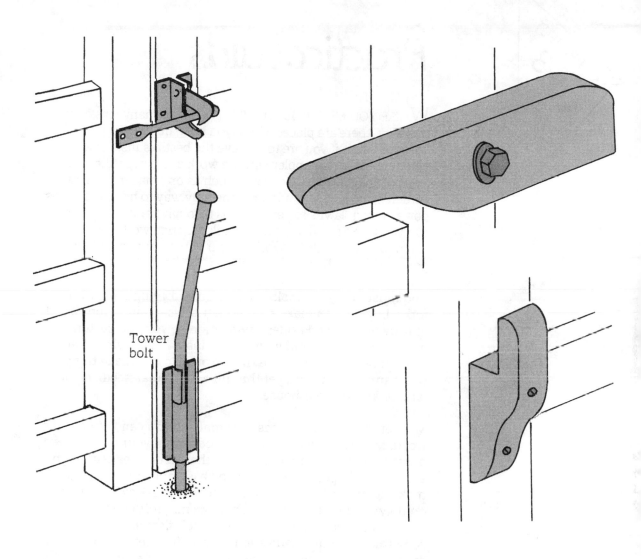

Tower
bolt

Practical aids

WHILE YOU MIGHT USE POWER TOOLS for many jobs on your property, there are places where you have no alternative but to use hand tools if you are to achieve the best results. For example, you might have to supplement the work of a power tiller with hand digging in awkward places such as on smaller plots, raised gardens, and boxes. In addition, the only way to bring the edges of power-mown lawns to perfection is through hand work. Not only can you make a variety of hand tools for such work, but you also can make other aids for work in your garden or to supplement power tools, such as supports for logs being chain-sawn.

You must buy some tools, such as good digging spades and forks, but you can make many other tools, mainly from wood, at little or no cost. Besides saving money, you can custom-make your tools to suit your needs, instead of having to accept something that is not quite right. You also can make things that cannot be bought, yet that fill a particular need on your land or around your house.

Most of these practical aids are small, so you can use scraps of wood. Many can be made from wood cut on your own property or salvaged from old buildings or other structures. Although accuracy is important in any wood assembly, most things you make do not call for precision woodworking. However, while a crudely constructed tool or appliance might function just as well as a better-made one, you will feel more satisfied with something soundly made and properly finished. Such a tool will encourage you to do better work than the crude improvisation.

Rakes Rakes of many sizes and types are easy to make, using nails for the tines of garden rakes and wood pegs for hay rakes. There are other rakelike tools you can make the same way, at top left of next page.

Garden rake You can make a basic garden rake any width you like. For general use, though, a hardwood rake 14 inches wide with tines 1½ inches apart is suitable, top right of next page.

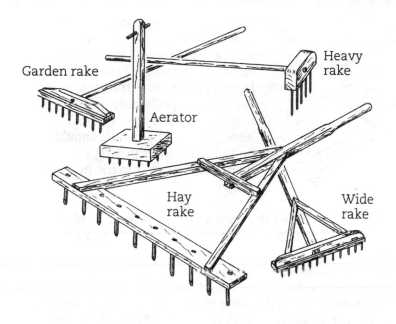

Garden rake

Aerator

Heavy rake

Hay rake

Wide rake

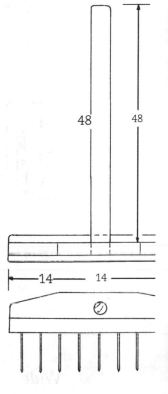

48 48

14 14

First, mark out the lower part, and drill undersize holes for 4-inch nails. How much undersize you drill the holes depends on the type of wood, but they should hold the nails tightly without splitting the wood when they are driven. Make the top piece to cover the nail heads (below).

Materials

2 heads	1 × 2 × 14
1 handle	50 × 1¼ diameter
9 4″ nails	

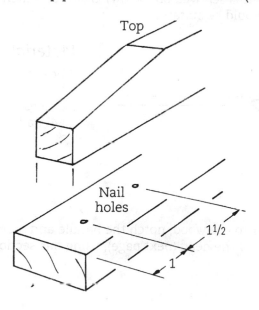

Top

Nail holes

1½

1

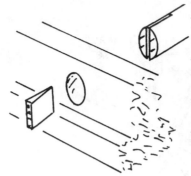

Next, drill the top piece for the handle. You can buy a handle, such as those used for brushes. Another alternative is to make one from a reasonably straight stick cut locally—preferably ash, hickory, or other springy wood. For a secure grip, the handle should be 1⅛ inches to 1⅜ inches diameter. Wedge it in the hole, as shown.

Join the parts of the rake head with screws driven upwards between the tines, as shown to the left. Four screws should be enough.

If you have to deal with narrow borders, you could make another narrower rake in the same way. However, if you want a much wider rake to gather leaves or lawn clippings, the handle will need bracing so the twisting load at the joint doesn't loosen or break the rake.

Wide rake   You can make a wide rake in the basic way but brace it with light steel strips screwed on (below). Strips of ⅛-inch-by-½-inch mild steel would be suitable.

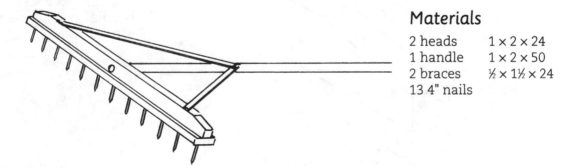

Materials

2 heads	1 x 2 x 24
1 handle	1 x 2 x 50
2 braces	½ x 1½ x 24
13 4" nails	

If you prefer to use wood, notch the handle and braces under the top part of the head (next page), using flat-section wood.

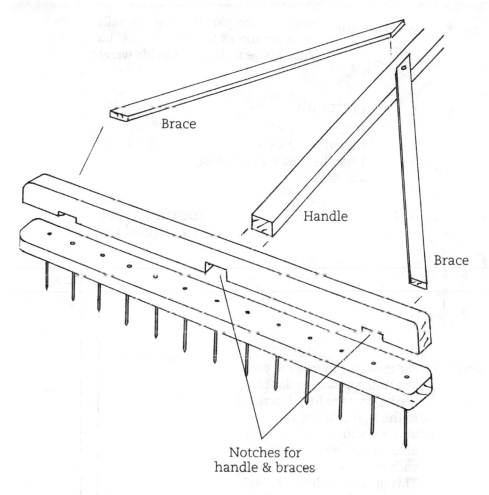

Brace

Handle

Brace

Notches for
handle & braces

Keep the handle flat to above the joint with the braces, then
work it to an elliptical section for the grip.

With an ordinary rake, you use a fairly gentle push-pull action
to get an even spread of fine, loose soil. On the other hand, if
the ground is hard and you want to use the rake to break into it
with a hitting action, it should have a shorter and heavier head.
The nails should be up to 6 inches long and arranged closer

Heavy rake

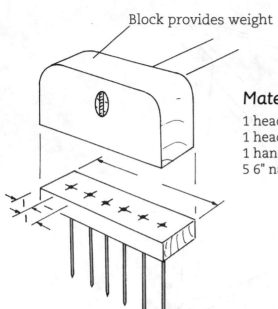

Block provides weight

together. The part holding the nails can be the same section as for a basic rake, but the thick block above it should provide weight.

Materials

1 head	1 × 2 × 8
1 head	2 × 4 × 8
1 handle	50 × 1¼ diameter
5 6" nails	

Perpendicular peg aids 2-handed grip

Aerator For aerating your lawn, you can make a tool similar to the heavy rake just described to the right. To use an aerator, you would bounce it all over the lawn or press in with your foot on hard parts. This action produces a mass of holes, which will ventilate the soil, encouraging the growth of grass and discouraging moss.

Materials

1 head	1 × 12 × 18
1 head	3 × 12 × 18
1 handle	2 × 2 × 36
1 grip	10 × ¾ diameter

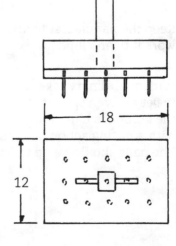

18

12

Arrange a pattern of nails in the base, and cut a heavy block to fit over it. The handle could be round or square, but it must be secure. Wedge it into the top piece as shown before screwing the base upward to it. A stout peg or piece of dowel rod across the top serves as your two-handed grip.

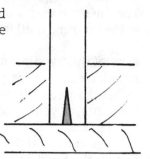

Hay rake

If you want to gather up long cut grass or hay you will need a large, light rake that will allow you to collect enough at each stroke without tiring. Traditional hay rakes were made of willow for lightness with reasonable strength. The example below has the head in one piece.

Materials

1 head	1¾ × 3 × 62
1 handle	2 × 2 × 40
2 handles	2 × 2 × 60
1 crossbar	2 × 2 × 24
10 tines	8 × ¾ diameter

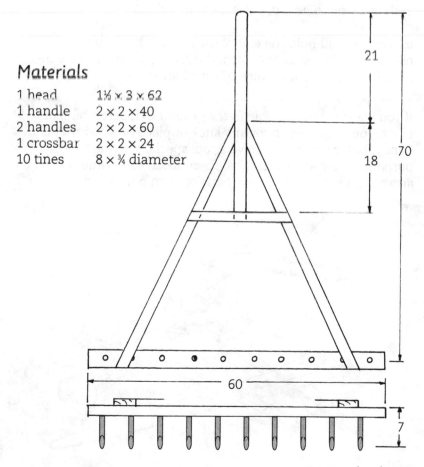

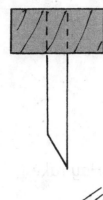

The tines are pieces of ¾-inch hardwood dowel rod. Cut slopes at the bottoms (left), and glue and wedge the tops.

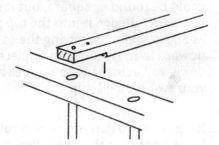

Parts of the handle could be round, natural rods up to 1½ inches diameter, flattened at the joints, or you could use square strips. Cut shallow notches in the handle sides to fit over the head and screw there.

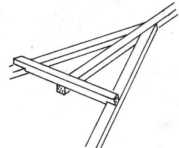

Cut the sides to fit against the straight handle and also screw there (left). Put a strip across to join the V sides and the end of the center piece. Add shallow notches in addition to screws at each crossing to help prevent movement.

In use, you will hold the end of the handle, but you also will reach to the crossbar to control the raking action, so be sure to round all parts within range of your hands.

Dibbers

If you want to make a hole in the ground to insert a bulb or plant, you might reach for any stick or piece of wood that is handy, but it is better to have a tool specially made for the purpose. There are a variety of these tools, sometimes called *dibbers* or *dibblers*, that you can make from hardwood.

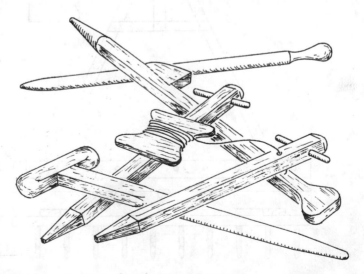

You have a choice of making your dibbers round or square. Round might seem the obvious choice, but keep in mind that a square piece can be pushed and twisted into the ground to produce a round hole. In addition, if you tilt the tool to make a tapered hole by twisting, the corners of the square dibber would be slightly better for scraping tight soil.

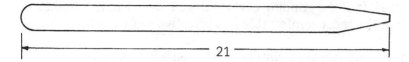

Consider the point of the dibber, too. If it is too fine and thin, it will soon break. A moderate taper and a flat end are better (above). If you turn a round end, let the tip be thick (below).

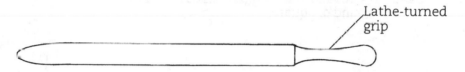

Lathe-turned grip

For most dibbers, you can use wood about 1¼ inches square or diameter. You can make larger holes by moving the tool around in the ground, but if you want to make a bigger hole with the first thrust you can shape a thicker dibber, reduced at the grip.

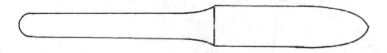

A plain, pointed stick with a rounded top might be all you need. If you make it long, such as the one shown below, you can use

Dowel grip

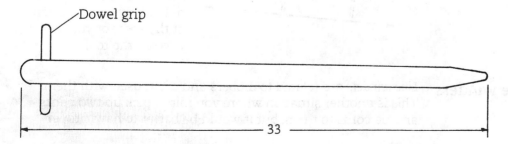

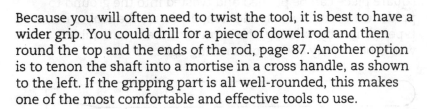

it without stooping. If you have the use of a lathe, you can turn the point and a grip (see page 87).

Because you will often need to twist the tool, it is best to have a wider grip. You could drill for a piece of dowel rod and then round the top and the ends of the rod, page 87. Another option is to tenon the shaft into a mortise in a cross handle, as shown to the left. If the gripping part is all well-rounded, this makes one of the most comfortable and effective tools to use.

Finally, you can get a similar grip by attaching shaped blocks on each side with waterproof glue and rounding them (at left).

If you want to avoid stooping and, instead, use your foot to push the tool into the hole, you can make the handle as long as a spade's (below). You can use any type of grip, and the shaft can be round or square.

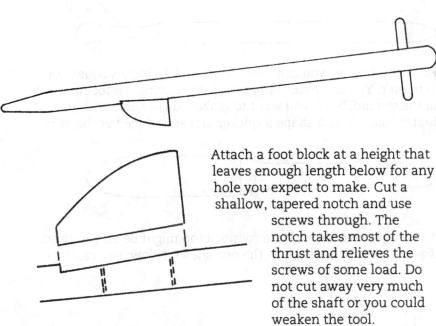

Attach a foot block at a height that leaves enough length below for any hole you expect to make. Cut a shallow, tapered notch and use screws through. The notch takes most of the thrust and relieves the screws of some load. Do not cut away very much of the shaft or you could weaken the tool.

Line winders   *Line winders* are related to dibbers and often used with them. This is another situation where you might pick up two sticks and tie cords to them, but it would be better to have proper tools. You need a simple peg at one end of the line and another peg arranged for winding the line.

The pegs could be made like dibbers, either without grips or with any of the handles suggested (below at left) You might use a dibber as a peg, but remember that you will probably want to use line and dibber at the same time. Line pegs need not be as thick as dibbers.

You can make a spool for winding the line in a variety of ways. One way is to glue pieces on each side of the peg and shape them (below at right).

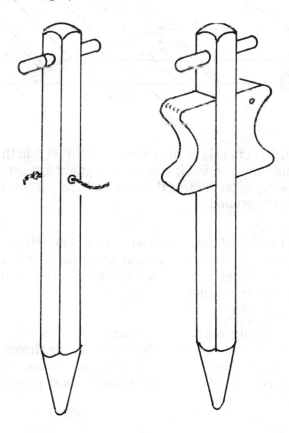

If this arrangement is a reasonable size, you can wind on all the cord you need. However, for more cord, make the shuttle wider, from a flat piece of wood screwed on (below to left), using a notch if the peg is round. Another, larger spool could be a frame of strips (below to right) about ⅜-inch-by-¾-inch section.

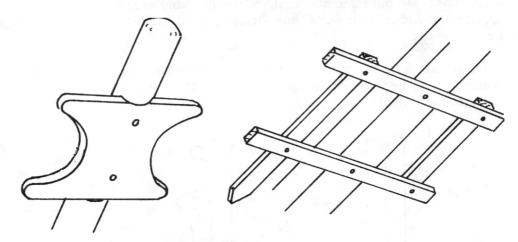

The winder is unlikely to turn when you thrust it in the ground and tension the line, but if you want to guard against this, you can screw a peg on the shuttle or extend one part of the frame to go into the ground.

Final touches

You can use any of these tools without treating them with paint or varnish, but they are small and easily mislaid. If you paint the handle ends bright red, you should be able to see them against any garden background.

Seedling protectors

When you plant rows of seeds, you need to know where they are and what is in each row. Then later, as the shoots appear, you probably will have to protect these vulnerable seedlings from hungry birds. You can make aids for both purposes (next page).

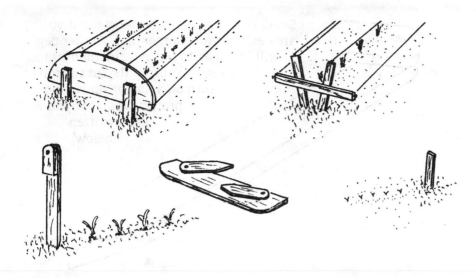

You can make something as simple as peg with the name of the crop written on it to place at the end of a row (below to left). Some gardeners cut the end of the peg and insert the seed packet (below to right), but will that survive wind and rain?

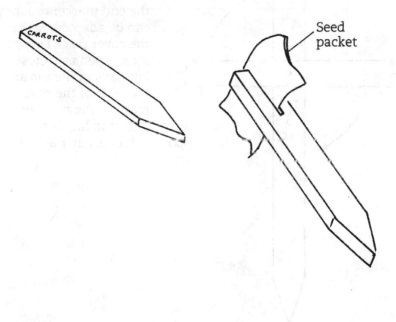

Seed
packet

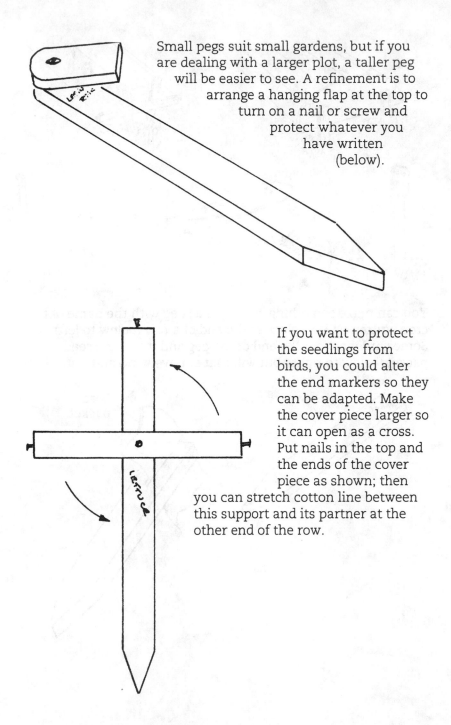

Small pegs suit small gardens, but if you are dealing with a larger plot, a taller peg will be easier to see. A refinement is to arrange a hanging flap at the top to turn on a nail or screw and protect whatever you have written (below).

If you want to protect the seedlings from birds, you could alter the end markers so they can be adapted. Make the cover piece larger so it can open as a cross. Put nails in the top and the ends of the cover piece as shown; then you can stretch cotton line between this support and its partner at the other end of the row.

If you want more than three strands of cotton, as you would if you need to protect more than one row, the simplest arrangement is a wide board on two pegs (below to left). If you are dealing with dense soil, you can let the pegs extend above the board so you can drive them in with a hammer. To make the arrangement compact for storage, arrange the pegs to pivot out of the way on screws (below to right).

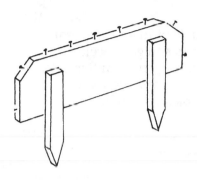 

If you think four strands of cotton will be enough and you prefer to use strips of wood, nail together a simple frame from pieces about ½-inch-by-1½-inch section (at right).

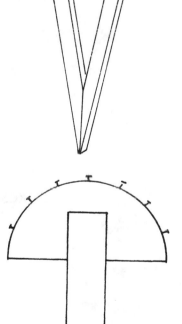

Although it is usual to drive nails into edges, you might prefer to drive them in the sides. In the latter case, the strained cotton  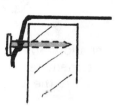 bears on the wood instead of pulling directly on the nail. This arrangement is preferable if you expect to put on a cover, as described later.

The best supports for cotton protectors are curved, either semicircular (at right) or half-elliptical (top of page 94), with rigid or pivoted supports. With these shapes, you can arrange as many nails as you want and the lower ones will be near the ground.

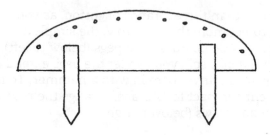

You can use curved supports if you want to arrange clear plastic sheeting to cover the seedlings and give a cold frame or greenhouse effect. Use string instead of cotton, in this case. Nails driven sideways into the supports will allow you to stretch the strings and arrange the plastic with little risk of tearing it.

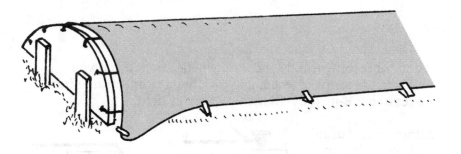

For a long row, you will have to arrange supports intermediately. Peg the plastic to the ground at the ends, and join it to the lower strings with clothespins.

Boxes In your garden or around your land, you will always have a need for boxes of different sorts (top of next page) They can be small for storage or growing seeds, larger for transporting potting plants, or very large for animal feeds or similar uses. Construction is the same; differences are in sizes. You can make boxes from rough wood or machined parallel pieces. In most cases, you will not need to cut elaborate joints. Nails or screws are sufficient fastenings, but they should be corrosion-resistant metal or galvanized steel.

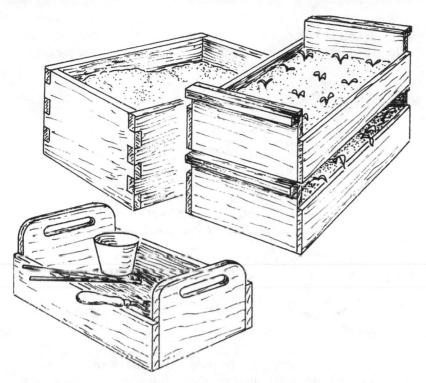

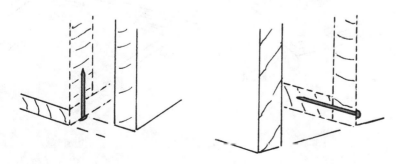

You can strengthen joints with dovetail nailing, but even then joints might force open under load, particularly if several inches of soil are pushing outward. A better option is to reinforce joints with strips of sheet metal (right).

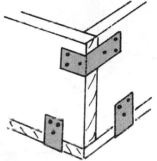

If you nail upward when constructing your box, the bottom of the box could push out in use (bottom left). It is much stronger to put the nail between the sides and bottom, as shown (bottom right). If you rabbet corners, you can nail both ways

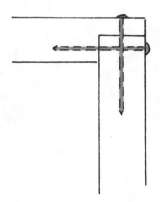

and the sides will not come apart unless the wood is broken (left). If you are using exterior plywood or solid wood, the most effective method is to notch the parts into each other (below).

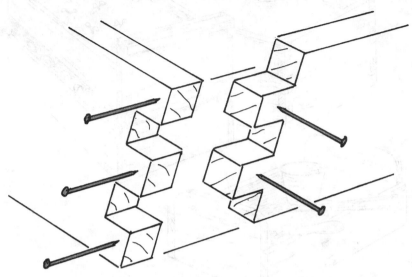

For most outdoor uses on your property, your boxes should have feet to keep the main area above the ground. Simple feet are strips under the length of the ends (below left). If you want to stack a pile of matching boxes, set the feet in far enough to fit loosely into the top of a lower box (below right).

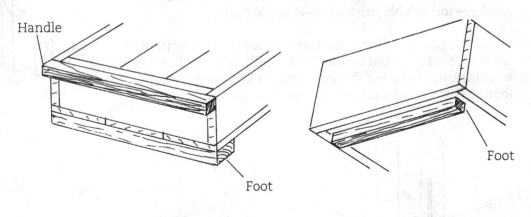

Handle

Foot

Foot

You can make simple lifting handles like feet (see page 96). If you raise the ends with their handles, inset feet allow stacking to leave air gaps.

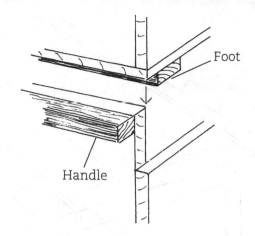

Foot

Handle

Strip handles give you a finger grip, but if a box is heavy, you will need to be able to put your hand through handles. One option is to cut through an end under a crossbar handle so you can put your fingers through (below left). Cut away at least 5 inches wide and about 1¾ inches deep, and well round all parts of the grip. An alternative is to shape thick ends to make lifting handles (below right).

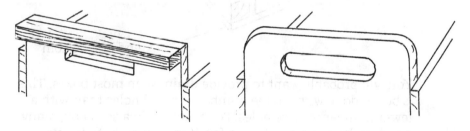

If your available wood for boxes is thin, such as offcuts of exterior plywood, you can strengthen it with framing. Plywood less than ½ inch thick could have 1-inch-square framing. It might be sufficient to frame the ends only, but you could put strips at the sides, with the box bottom extended to nail under the lower ones (top of next page). More strips could form feet across under the ends, or you could just put blocks under the corners. External framing of this type provides grips all around and leaves a smooth interior.

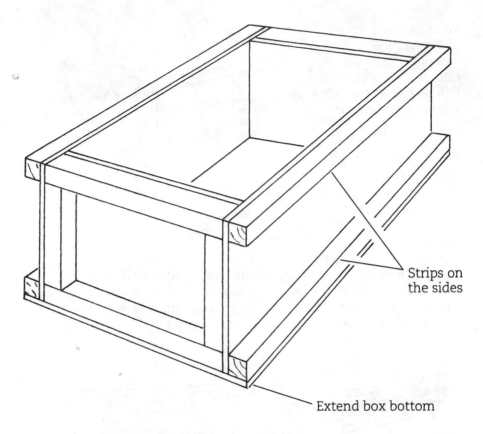

Strips on the sides

Extend box bottom

You will probably want to provide drainage in most boxes. This is better done with a large number of small holes than with a fewer number of large holes. For example, in a seed box, many ⅜-inch holes are better than a few ¾-inch ones, both for even drainage and to limit the risk of anything falling through.

Plant supports

Many things you grow will benefit from a variety of supports (top of opposite page). In some cases, a support can be a plain post, varying from a stick or cane no more than ½ inch across to a substantial piece of 2-inch-square, or larger, wood. You can often pick up a suitable piece of wood, but it is worthwhile preparing a stock of supports in advance. This could be an interesting occupation out of the growing season.

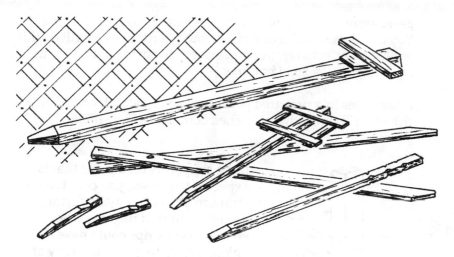

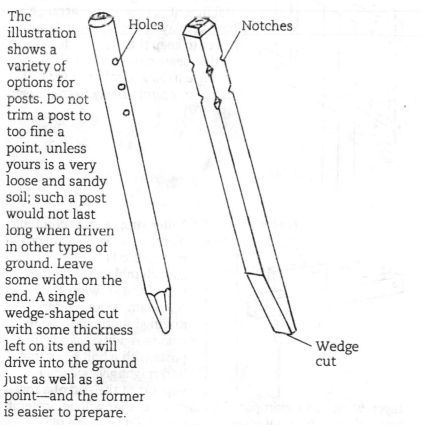

The illustration shows a variety of options for posts. Do not trim a post to too fine a point, unless yours is a very loose and sandy soil; such a post would not last long when driven in other types of ground. Leave some width on the end. A single wedge-shaped cut with some thickness left on its end will drive into the ground just as well as a point—and the former is easier to prepare.

Holes

Notches

Wedge cut

Bevel around the top of a post to reduce the risk of splitting. You could use a knife or a chisel, but a Surform tool will do this easily and effectively. (A mallet is less likely to split a post than pounding with a steel hammer.)

A few holes in a prepared post allow you to attach cord without risk of it slipping down. Notched corners serve a similar purpose.

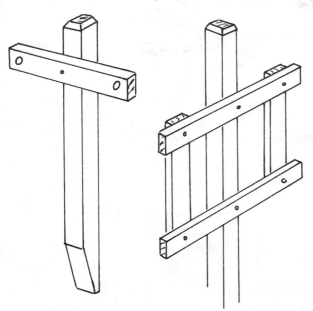

If the support is for a plant that is expected to spread, you could nail a strip across to allow tying further out (far left), but that might not be enough. Two strips could have linking pieces to give you plenty of attachment places as you arrange a floral display or spread fruit. If you expect to keep this support for another season, the parts can pivot on single nails and fold flat for storage in a similar way to trellis (see page 107).

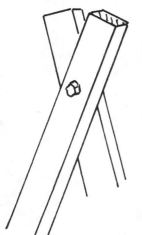

Gusset

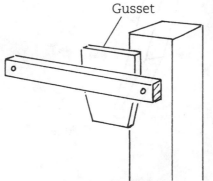

Taller supports for climbing plants or vegetables might be expected to take considerable weight by the end of the growing season. Allow ample length for driving into the ground to ensure rigidity. Two lighter posts with a bolt pivot (far left) might give steadier support at the end of a row.

If you want to support parallel lines, a crossbar will be firmer if you include a triangular gusset, which could be made of exterior plywood.

If you will be erecting ropes from ground to top supports for plants to climb, prepared pegs provide more secure anchorage than odd sticks picked up (far right), which might allow ropes to loosen disastrously when plants are well-advanced. You could use top ropes between supports, but light battens will better resist sagging under load.

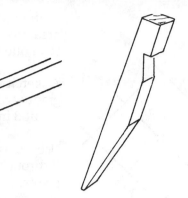

Trellises

The diamond pattern of trelliswork looks good even when you do not have anything climbing on it . Trellises can be supported vertically against a wall or on posts. You might need to tie some plants to a trellis, but others will entwine or cling with tendrils. Out of season, you can compress the trellis sideways for compact storage.

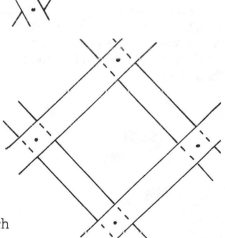

Wood should usually be between ⅛ inch and ⅜ inch thick and ¾ inch to 1¼ inches wide, depending on the expected load. Plan for a trellis with a square pattern, but, in use, you can expand it to diamonds in either direction to allow adjustment of size or appearance. Squares at 5-inch

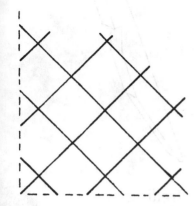

centers would suit most needs. If you want to cover a large area, two or more sections would be easier to make and handle than one large one.

A sketch with single lines will show how lengths of battens are graduated at a corner (left). Allow ends of strips to extend about 3 inches.

Use a single galvanized nail at the center of each crossing. Take it through and clench the end. In this way, the nails act as pivots, which allows you to fold strips against each other for storage. Let the nail go through up to ½ inch. With an iron block supporting the head, hammer the end to a curve over a spike (below left). Withdraw the spike and bury the point in the wood (below right).

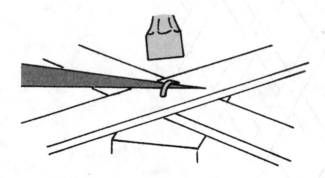
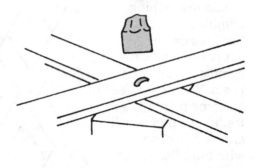

Sawbuck

A traditional-style trestle or *sawbuck*, while primitive in style, is still the most favored choice of homesteaders for holding logs while sawing. The sawbuck shown on facing page supports logs at thigh height, which is convenient for using either a handsaw or a chain saw.

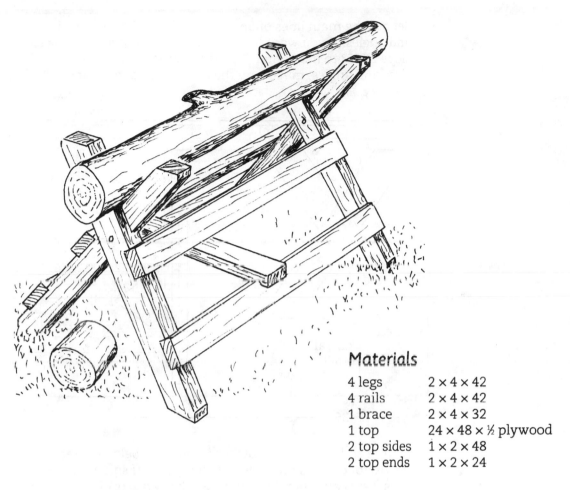

Materials

4 legs	2 × 4 × 42
4 rails	2 × 4 × 42
1 brace	2 × 4 × 32
1 top	24 × 48 × ½ plywood
2 top sides	1 × 2 × 48
2 top ends	1 × 2 × 24

The sawbuck has a broad base for stability, and you can add a top to form a table or light bench. All parts are 2-inch-by-4-inch section, and the wood need not be planed. Construction is with bolts and screws. Notch joints, all ½ inch deep, provide rigidity. (A greater depth would weaken the wood.) Use glue in all joints. Nails instead of screws would have to be long and plentiful to equal the strength of screws.

Set out the main lines of an end view (below) to obtain sizes and angles. If you want to set a machine to cut angles, the sides slope at 35° to horizontal. This is not crucial, but if you alter sizes and angles, make sure the feet spread enough for stability.

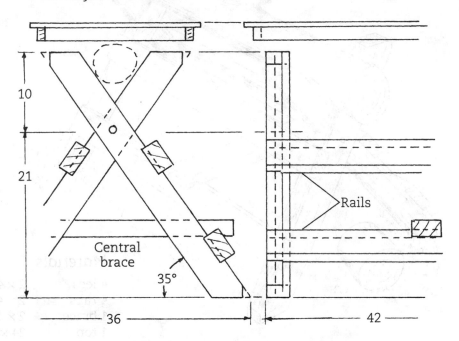

Cut the end angles and notches in the legs (below). To reduce the risk of corners breaking out, cut them off square to the ends. Bevel all around the ends. Fit the two sets of legs together with ½-inch bolts at the centers.

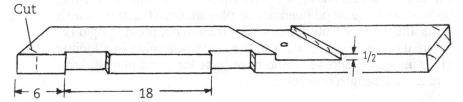

Make four identical rails (top of facing page), notched ½ inch deep at the ends. Close-fitting notched joints contribute to rigidity of the trestle. If possible, cut mating parts so they have to be forced together by hammering or squeezing with clamps.

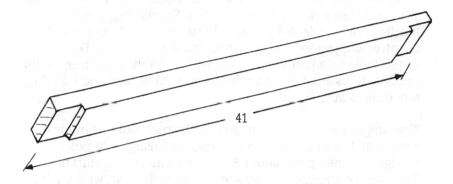

41

The sawbuck might be strong enough without the central brace, but joints could loosen after prolonged use and this piece gives extra strength. Cut it with notches to fit on the bottom rails, as shown below, and screw it in place.

You could make a tabletop about 24 inches by 48 inches to drop over the corners of the trestle. The simplest arrangement is a piece of ½-inch waterproof plywood with 1-inch-by-2-inch strips added like box sides below it. If you want a more substantial top to use as a bench, you could make it of solid wood boards on a stiffer framing.

If you want to confine stock to a small area or erect a temporary fence, you can use several hurdles together, with their legs thrust or driven into the ground. They are easy to move elsewhere or to rearrange. Hurdles have been made in many ways and from several materials. The gate type, described here, is the traditional one.

Hurdles

You rarely use just one hurdle. If you do make a number of them, standardize on size so you can group them together to form a compound or fence. They need not all be made of the same sections of wood to use in this way.

You could use sawn sections of wood. For the suggested hurdles, this is 1-inch-by-3-inch hardwood. For larger hurdles or softwood, you would have to increase the section. For general use on a homestead, you will probably have uses for up to six hurdles at a time, so scheme your materials and building schedule to suit.

The suggested hurdle design (shown below) could be made of sawn wood, but construction is described using split poles. Straight-grained poles about 3 inches diameter are suitable. They will be strongest if you are able to split them with wedges, as the division will follow grain lines. Of course, sawing the poles in half gives a cleaner face surface and should provide ample strength.

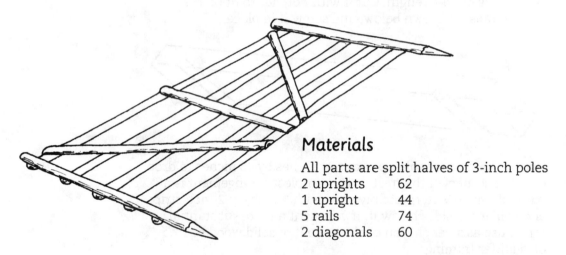

Materials

All parts are split halves of 3-inch poles

2 uprights	62
1 upright	44
5 rails	74
2 diagonals	60

Overall sizes might depend on available poles, but the suggested dimensions produce a useful hurdle, not too heavy or unwieldy to move (next page).

Make the uprights to project about 3 inches at the top, and bevel the end to reduce the risk of splitting if you drive the post with a hammer. Make the lower ends pointed.

Cut the rails a little too long at first so you can trim them after fitting. The diagonals and center upright also should be long enough to allow for cutting after assembly. Arrange the rails so

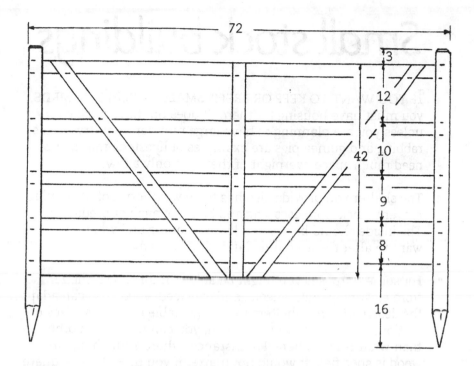

spaces diminish towards the bottom to provide more resistance to smaller animals trying to break through.

It should be strong enough to make each joint with a single, thick, galvanized nail long enough to go through and project about 1 inch, so the end can be turned back into the wood

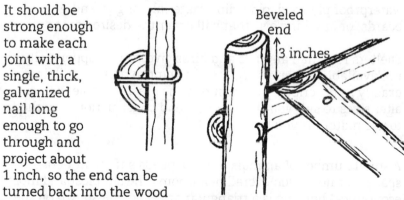

Beveled end

3 inches

(right). Arrange the diagonals to come close to the uprights (far right). Although exceptional precision is unnecessary in a hurdle, you should check squareness during assembly and nail through every crossing to give maximum strength. To complete the hurdle, trim off the ends and remove any raggedness.

Small stock buildings

IF YOU WANT TO KEEP OR BREED SMALL ANIMALS OR BIRDS, you must have housing for them. It does not have to be big, unless you are planning to have large numbers. Poultry, ducks, rabbits, and guinea pigs are examples of livestock that do not need much space overnight, if there are only a few.

The shelter you provide also has to be weatherproof. It should prevent stock from escaping and be proof against predators. The inside should be accessible for cleaning and you might want to alter the accommodation if you change uses.

For some purposes you might be able to improvise a shelter from existing panels, sheets, and salvaged wood. You can adapt the design of some shelters to suit available materials. Sizes of sections of framing are not crucial; you can used wood other than what is listed here. For instance, where 1½-inch-square wood is specified, it would not matter if you used 2-inch-square or even 2-inch-by-3-inch wood. In a small structure, wood of available sizes will almost certainly be more than strong enough. Similarly, a satisfactory covering can be made of waterproof plywood, old siding material, tongue-and-groove boards, or anything else that will cover the desired area.

Shelters for small animals and birds give you an opportunity to use available materials. You might want to make a building exactly as described, but most designs are adaptable. You can alter sizes to suit your needs or amend constructional methods to use materials you have already.

Small ark

A small number of animals or birds needs sufficient floor space, but not much overall headroom. The simplest and most economical housing is a triangular ark. The one shown on the next page would suit a variety of small livestock. There is access through a pop hole with a clearance about 6 inches square, but you could alter this, if necessary. Ventilation can be arranged through a high opening covered with wire mesh, with an outside flap. The ark is shown without a floor; it is intended

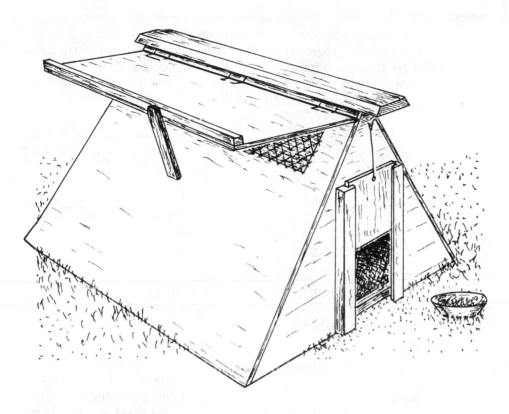

Materials

2 ends from	24 × 48 × ½ plywood
2 side panels	30 × 30 × ½ plywood
1 pop hole cover	7½ × 8½ × ½ plywood
1 ventilator cover	12 × 30 × ½ plywood
1 ventilator cover	2 × 30 × ½ plywood
8 frames	1½ × 1½ × 30
1 ridge	2 × 3 × 30
1 ridge cover	1 × 5 × 36
2 pop hole guides	½ × 1½ × 18
2 pop hole guides	⅝ × 1 × 18
1 ventilator cover edge	1 × 1 × 30
1 ventilator strut	½ × 1½ × 12

to be placed directly on the ground. If you want a floor, use a piece of plywood, an assembly of boards, or an arrangement of slats. The ark is light enough to lift for cleaning or moving to another site.

Construction is with ½-inch exterior plywood on framing. Parts can be nailed together. Frame parts butt against each other, so there is no need for cut joints. As shown below, there is a pop hole in one end, ventilation at one side, and a cover strip to provide weather protection at the top.

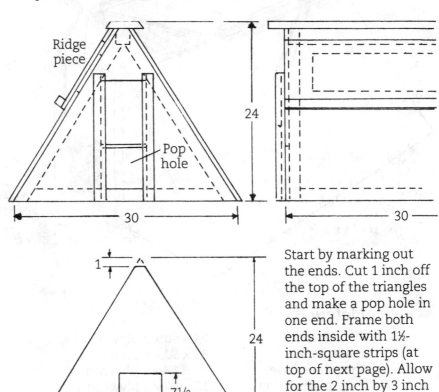

Start by marking out the ends. Cut 1 inch off the top of the triangles and make a pop hole in one end. Frame both ends inside with 1½-inch-square strips (at top of next page). Allow for the 2 inch by 3 inch ridge piece at the top, which will fit in notches. The framing is shown going across the pop hole at the bottom. You could cut it away or provide a ramp if you are dealing with very small animals or birds, but leaving it in provides rigidity.

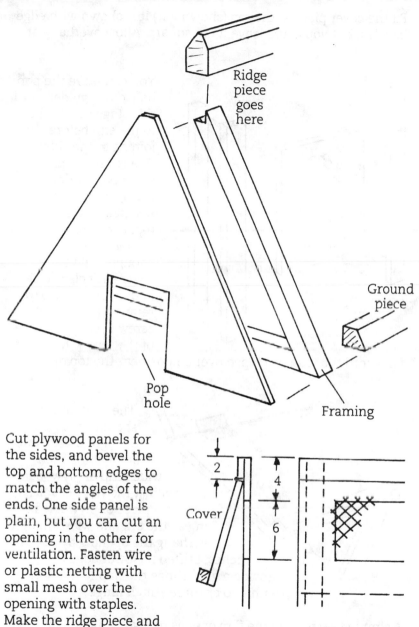

Ridge piece goes here

Ground piece

Pop hole

Framing

2

Cover

4

6

Cut plywood panels for the sides, and bevel the top and bottom edges to match the angles of the ends. One side panel is plain, but you can cut an opening in the other for ventilation. Fasten wire or plastic netting with small mesh over the opening with staples. Make the ridge piece and the ground pieces (above) next, with angles to match the slopes of the ends. Join the side panels to these pieces and to the ends.

Small stock buildings 111

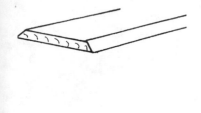

Fit the cover piece at the top (shown left) It is shown with edge beveled, but you could leave it cut square. Allow overhang at the ends.

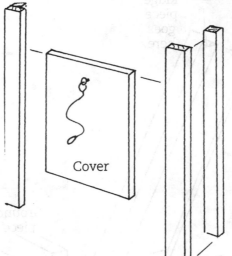

Cover

You can leave the pop hole cover guides until this stage or add them to the end before joining to the sides. The cover is a piece of plywood, overlapping the opening by at least ¾ inch at the sides and top. Each guide is made with a piece thick enough to give the cover easy clearance and an outer strip to retain it (far left). Put a screw eye at the center of the top of the cover for a cord that can be looped over a hook near the top of the ark end.

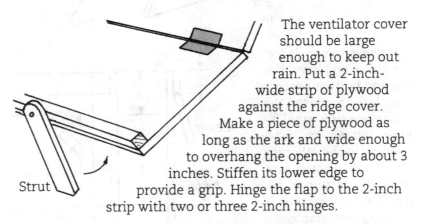

Strut

The ventilator cover should be large enough to keep out rain. Put a 2-inch-wide strip of plywood against the ridge cover. Make a piece of plywood as long as the ark and wide enough to overhang the opening by about 3 inches. Stiffen its lower edge to provide a grip. Hinge the flap to the 2-inch strip with two or three 2-inch hinges.

A simple way to prop the flap open is to pivot a light strut near the center of the stiffening piece. Make its length to suit the amount of ventilation you require.

If you finish the ark with paint or preservative, be sure to let that and any of its vapor dry out before introducing stock to the ark.

If you want to hatch chickens from eggs under a broody hen in the traditional way, you need a small house with an attached run for the chickens. This coop has a square house and a detachable run.

Chicken coop

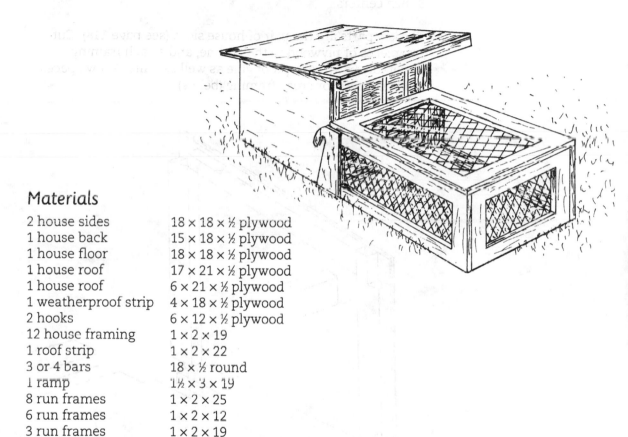

Materials

2 house sides	18 × 18 × ½ plywood
1 house back	15 × 18 × ½ plywood
1 house floor	18 × 18 × ½ plywood
1 house roof	17 × 21 × ½ plywood
1 house roof	6 × 21 × ½ plywood
1 weatherproof strip	4 × 18 × ½ plywood
2 hooks	6 × 12 × ½ plywood
12 house framing	1 × 2 × 19
1 roof strip	1 × 2 × 22
3 or 4 bars	18 × ½ round
1 ramp	1½ × 3 × 19
8 run frames	1 × 2 × 25
6 run frames	1 × 2 × 12
3 run frames	1 × 2 × 19

The hen will be restricted by bars, which can be lifted out. The house has a floor, but the run is open to the ground. When not used for its primary purpose, this chicken coop could house small animals.

Construction is with 1-inch-by-2-inch strips. The house is covered with ½-inch exterior plywood. Sizes are suggested, but this is a project where sizes can be altered easily at the planning stage. So the restraining dowel rods are accessible for lifting, there is a hinged section of the roof. Three bars should be enough for a normal hen, but for a bantam or another kind of small bird, you might find it better to have four bars at 3-inch centers.

The key parts are the pair of house sides (see page 118). Cut two pieces of plywood to the outline, and attach framing, preferably with waterproof glue as well as nails. Allow spaces at the corners for cross-framing (below).

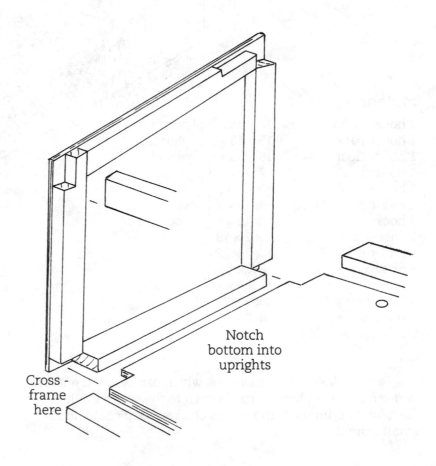

Notch
bottom into
uprights

Cross-
frame
here

At the top front corners allow space for the crosspiece to hold the dowel rod bars (below).

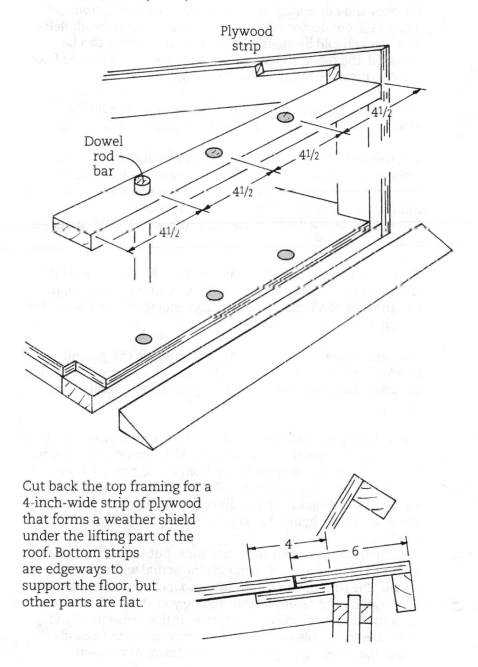

Plywood strip

Dowel rod bar

4 1/2

4 1/2

4 1/2

4 1/2

Cut back the top framing for a 4-inch-wide strip of plywood that forms a weather shield under the lifting part of the roof. Bottom strips are edgeways to support the floor, but other parts are flat.

4

6

Rods do not go
all the way through

Join the sides with strips across and prepare the bottom plywood to notch round the uprights. Drill the front top rail for the bars and put matching holes in the floor and bottom rail (page 115), but do not take them the whole way through (left). The holes should be an easy fit on the rods so they can be removed and replaced without trouble. You can leave the floor loose so it can be removed for cleaning.

Fit the back plywood panel. Check that, so far, the house assembly is rigid, square, and without twist.

The roof should overhang about 1½ inches at the back and sides. Fit the weatherproof strip, and make the main panel of the roof to come up to its center. Glue and nail these parts. The lifting part of the roof should extend far enough to protect the front of the house. Make it the full width with a strip under its edge.

Two 3-inch hinges on top should be enough, but there is little thickness for screwing, and it would be better to rivet them. Cut the bars of a length to stand high enough above the rail for gripping.

The house floor will be about 1½ inches above the ground. Chickens will need a ramp, which could be a tapered piece of solid wood or a piece of plywood supported by a solid-wood rod.

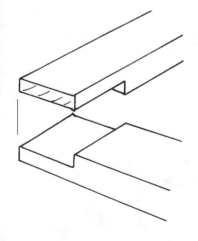

The run is assembled from frames covered with wire netting. Corner joints are halving joints (left). Make two matching sides. Their ends will come close to the front of the house (shown on the next page). The end in this illustration is shown 16 inches long, but you might need to adjust this slightly so it matches the width of the house, to keep the sides parallel.

The top frame is shown 18 inches wide, but, again, that size might have to be altered to match the actual width of the house. The run top rests in position so it can be lifted off. To locate it and to prevent it from sliding you should fix a block underneath at each corner, but delay fitting these until you assemble the whole run and can position them to fit easily inside the other parts, yet prevent excessive movement.

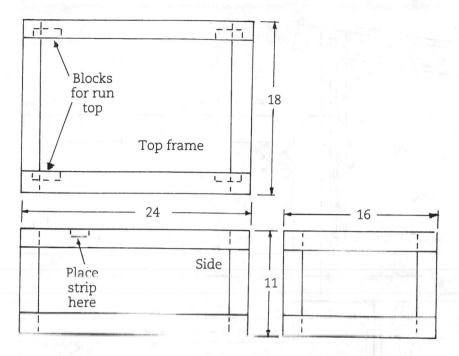

Use wire or plastic netting not larger than 1-inch mesh. Cut this to overlap the framing about ¾ inch, and fix it inside with plenty of staples. Hammer any wire ends into the wood.

So the run can be moved easily, it is arranged to hook onto the sides of the house (shown at top of next page). Cut two plywood hook shapes using the pattern provided (shown at bottom of next page) and screw them to the run sides. You could make the pegs on the house from ½-inch dowel rods set into holes, or you could drive stout screws—14 gauge by 1½-inch roundhead screws would be suitable.

Screw the end run between the sides. Put a strip across near the house end, but far enough away to miss the positioning blocks on the run top. You could nail it between or make notched joints. Check the length of the piece in position so you are able to lift and hook the run easily onto its pegs.

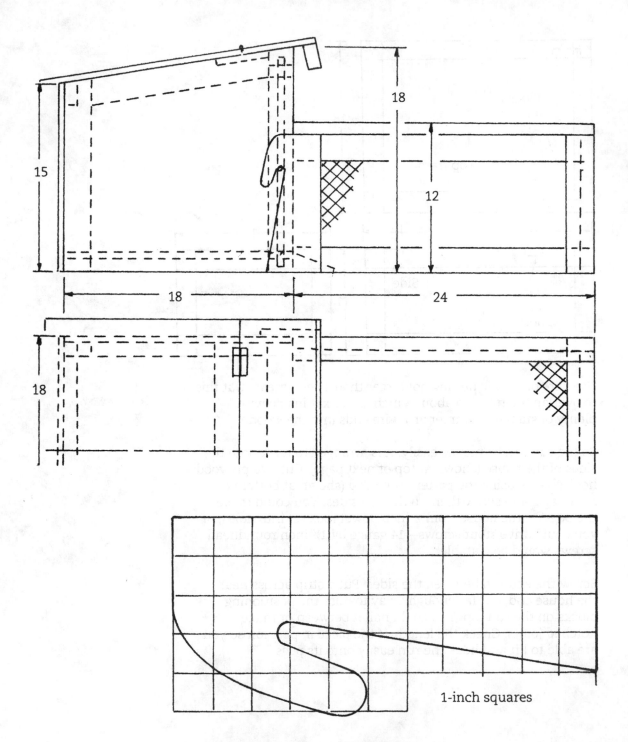

15

18

18

24

18

12

1-inch squares

118 Outdoor Projects for the Country Home

If children want to keep pet rabbits, guinea pigs (cavies), or other small animals, the accommodation provided is often crude. This hutch shown below has an uneven ridged roof to give protection and avoid the box-on-edge appearance of many examples. The sizes suggested (page 120) should suit two or three small animals that can make a bed in reasonable seclusion, while still providing enough space for them to run around.

Rabbit hutch

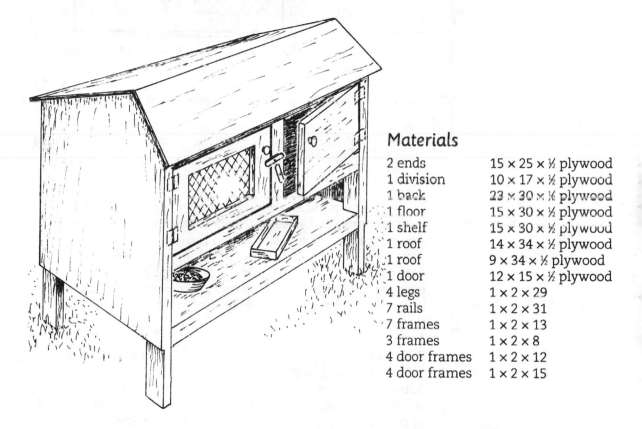

Materials

2 ends	15 × 25 × ½ plywood
1 division	10 × 17 × ½ plywood
1 back	23 × 30 × ½ plywood
1 floor	15 × 30 × ½ plywood
1 shelf	15 × 30 × ½ plywood
1 roof	14 × 34 × ½ plywood
1 roof	9 × 34 × ½ plywood
1 door	12 × 15 × ½ plywood
4 legs	1 × 2 × 29
7 rails	1 × 2 × 31
7 frames	1 × 2 × 13
3 frames	1 × 2 × 8
4 door frames	1 × 2 × 12
4 door frames	1 × 2 × 15

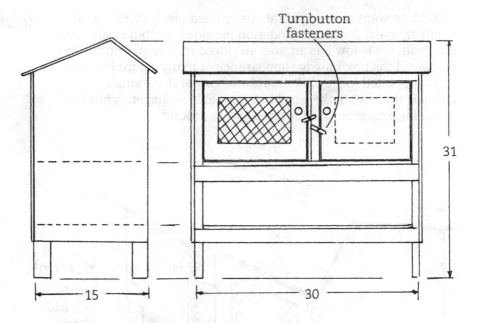

Doors to both parts allow for cleaning or removing animals. A shelf underneath, closed at the back and ends, gives you storage space and serves to stiffen the legs.

Construction is with 1-inch-by-2-inch strips on ½-inch exterior plywood. Cut joints are not necessary in most parts that come in contact with the covering; plywood, nailed and glued on, provides ample strength.

Start by marking out and cutting the plywood for one end (shown on facing page). Mark on it the position of framing. Allow for actual sizes of wood, and remember that planed wood will be less than its nominal size. The ridge piece should be central under the apex, but because of the uneven slopes, it will not be central between frame parts. At both eaves allow for inner surfaces of lengthwise parts to be at full depth, letting outer edges of slots come as they will, which will be less than 2 inches deep. Complete this end and make the opposite end a pair to it. The framing extends as legs below the plywood. You might want to alter the overall height by lengthening the legs.

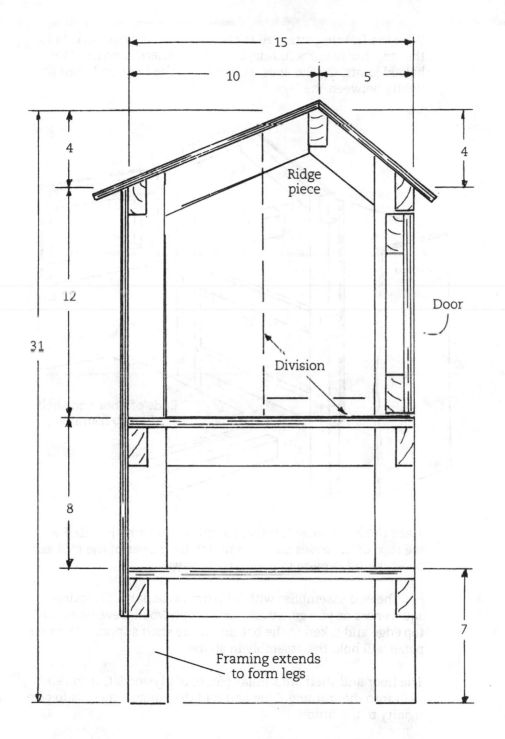

Ridge piece

Door

Division

Framing extends to form legs

Small stock buildings 121

With the framing attached to the plywood, arrange sockets for the lengthwise parts full-depth (below). There is no need for halved joints. On the ends, supports for the floor and shelf fit tightly between the legs.

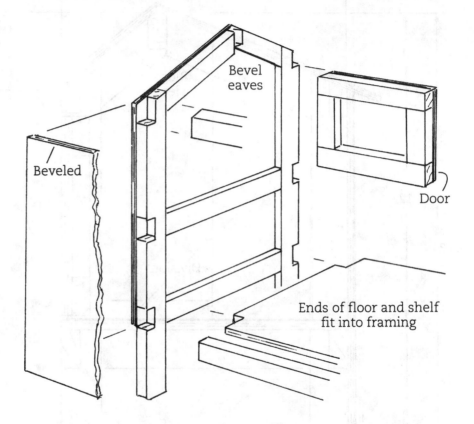

Bevel eaves

Beveled

Door

Ends of floor and shelf fit into framing

Make the lengthwise framing pieces all the same length. Bevel the tops of the eaves pieces to match the slopes of the roof and bevel the ridge piece to match both ways.

Join the end assemblies with all lengthwise parts. Checking squareness as you go, attach the rear plywood, beveled at the top edge and taken to the bottom of the shelf support. The rear panel will hold the assembly in shape.

The floor and shelf are similar pieces of plywood. Cut the ends to fit into the framing. Glue and nail the supporting rails to give rigidity to the hutch.

You can position the division where you like, but having the run surface of plywood in the center should be satisfactory (page 120). Allow about 6 inches for the animals to pass behind the division. Cut the shape similar to the front part of an end above floor level, allowing for the gap at the rear. Frame the edges in a similar way to the end, with notches onto the lengthwise parts, except leave the rear vertical edge unframed and round its edge. Join the division to the floor and the lengthwise framing.

Cut the roof panels to meet closely along the ridge and to overhang 1 inch at the ends and the eaves. When you attach the roof panels, make sure the ridge joint is waterproof. If the plywood edges do not meet closely, fill any gaps with stopping or waterproof glue mixed with sawdust.

Make the door to the sleeping compartment by framing plywood so it fits easily into the opening. The door to the run is a frame covered inside with wire netting. For strength, make this door with glued and screwed halving joints. Although plywood gives strength to the framing of the other door, you might want to halve the framing joints, as well.

You could let hinges into the door edges for neatness, but on this hutch it would be satisfactory to put 2-inch hinges on the surface. The doors could be arranged to swing whichever way you want. Catches at the opening edges must resist animals pushing against them. You could use store-bought catches, but the simplest fasteners are turnbuttons (page 120) made from strips of wood, turning on screws with washers under their heads. Provide handles or knobs for pulling the doors.

Small stock shed

If you keep animals, you need to provide shelter—either for them or for feed and equipment. If you are concerned with such animals as sheep and goats the building does not have to be large, but even if floor space need not be very big, you will want to be able to stand up inside.

This shed shown below has standing headroom for most of its area (on next page). The suggested door is divided to make a stable-type door, so you can leave the top open for ventilation or observation. Additional ventilation can be arranged high on the side, with a flap to close when necessary. You could put windows there, but they are inappropriate for the proposed use.

Materials

End framing

4 pieces	2 × 2 × 86
8 pieces	2 × 2 × 74
2 pieces	2 × 2 × 40
1 piece	1 × 2 × 74
2 pieces	1 × 4 × 74
1 piece	1 × 4 × 36

Side framing

7 pieces	2 × 2 × 98
8 pieces	2 × 2 × 86

Flap

2 pieces	2 × 2 × 98
4 pieces	2 × 2 × 16

Doors

4 pieces	2 × 2 × 38
3 pieces	2 × 2 × 48
3 pieces	2 × 2 × 30

Roof

20 pieces	1 × 6 × 84
(or equivalent area)	
4 pieces	2 × 2 × 96

Cladding

1 × 6 shiplap boards
1 × 6 plain boards for doors

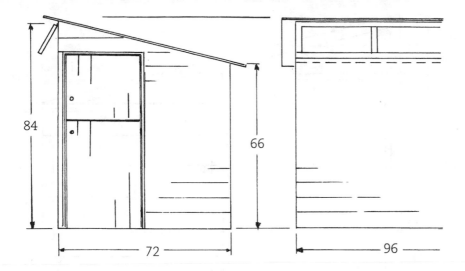

Construction is sectional. You can make the parts in your shop
and bolt them together on site. Shiplap boards on framing are
described here, but you could use vertical boards, plywood, or a
mixture of covering if you want to make use of what material
you have available. If the building is sectional, you will be able
to take it apart to store or to move it. Individual sections can be
carried by two people and the whole disassembled shed can be
loaded on a truck. You can arrange the building to stand
directly on the ground, or you can place it on a concrete base or
a wooden floor.

Decide at which end you want the door, and make that part
first (shown on page 126), then use it for settling related sizes
on other parts. This first frame has all covering boarding level
with the edges, including the doorway. As shown, the final door
clearance is about 32 inches wide and 71 inches high. Check if
this will suit your needs. You can place the inner upright where
you want it.

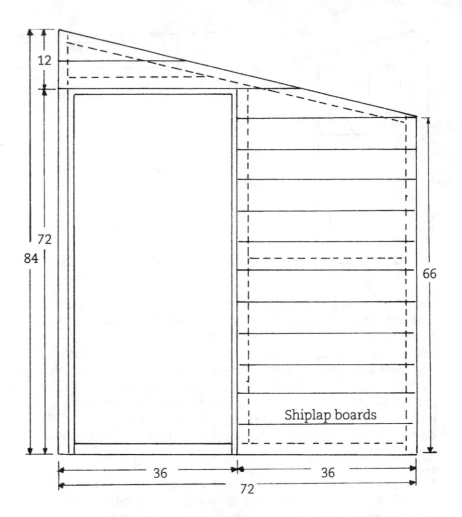

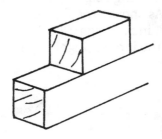

When the end is assembled, the covering will provide some strength to the framing, but you should make adequate joints. You have a choice of joining methods at the corners and along the edges. You could nail, but drilling will reduce the risk of splitting. It might be better to locate parts against blocks, as shown.

You could reinforce nailed joints with thin sheet metal gussets nailed on (below left). Halving joints give accurate positioning, as well as strength, at corners or intermediately (below right). At the top of the doorway, cut the strip to fit into the jointed corner (below left).

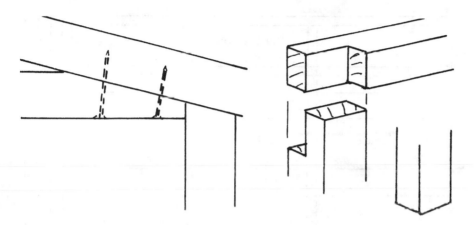

Assemble the framing on a flat surface and check squareness. The drawing shows shiplap boards about 1 inch by 6 inches, nailed on, starting at the bottom (top of facing page). Cut off the boards level at the doorway as well as at the outside edges. Fill up to the same thickness with a strip at the outside edge of the doorway. Put doorframe pieces at the sides and top of the doorway (at right).

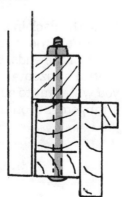

Doorframe pieces

Outside edge of doorway

Make the opposite end to match the door end, but carry the middle rail right across and put boarding all over.

The framing of the side has to fit inside the end framing, so the covering must extend over that. Check the amount on the ends. Although this should be about 3 inches, your wood sections might be slightly different.

Covering

Make the framing for the high side (below) to match the height of the edge of the ends and with allowance for the extended covering boards. Fit the shiplap boarding, leaving the ventilation gap at the top. Make up the width and thickness with boards at each end and along the top.

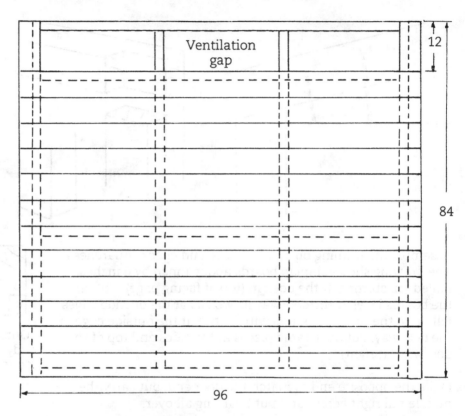

Make the back in a similar way, with extended boarding at each end, but without ventilation. Make the height to match the low edges of the ends. It should be strong enough to arrange one central horizontal rail, but you could have more, particularly if you will want to support shelving or make other internal arrangements on that wall.

The flap to cover the ventilation gap is a simple covered frame as long as the high side (below). Hinge it to the side (shown at right) with four 3-inch hinges. In use, you can prop the flap open with a stick or use a strut intended for an opening window.

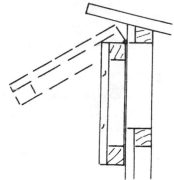

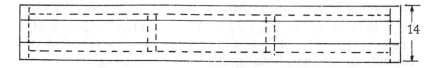

You can make and fit the doors while the end frame is flat or you can leave the work until the shed is assembled. If you do not want a two-part door, make a single one the same way as the bottom part.

Make the frames for the doors with ample clearance all around and between them.

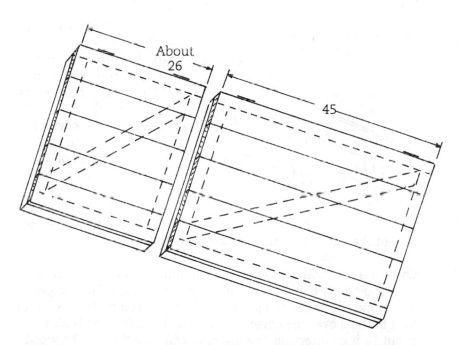

Allow for the thickness of hinges and enough space at ground level. Have the diagonal struts rising from the hinge side to resist any tendency to sag. You can hinge the doors on either side to suit your needs. The covering is shown as plain boards arranged vertically, but you could use shiplap, tongue-and-groove boards, or plywood.

The doors are fairly heavy, so you should use 4-inch or 5-inch butt hinges set into the edges or large T-hinges on the surface. Arrange a bolt inside the top door to link it to the bottom one so they can be swung as one. Fit a door lock or a hasp and staple for a padlock on the lower door, and knobs or handles on both doors. The bottom door will close against the lower framing bar, but you should also provide a stop strip at the edge (see page 127), either the full height or for a short distance at the door overlap.

Assemble the walls with ⅜-inch carriage bolts (see page 127). Drill the ends for bolts at about 18-inch intervals, but do not drill the adjoining uprights until you put the corners together and can drill through. Have the walls assembled squarely on a reasonably flat surface. Stand back and look for twist.

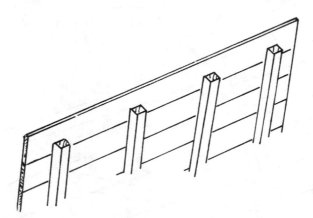

The roof could be ½-inch plywood, but the plan calls for plain boards laid from front to back with an overhang all around of 3 inches or more. Make the crosswise strips to fit inside the tops of the walls. Nail the roof securely to the wall framing.

Cover the roof with tarred or other roofing material, laid so any overlapping joints will shed water down the slope. Turn under all around the edges and secure with large-head nails. If you nail light battens over the covering material, from front to back at about 18-inch intervals, the material will stay close to the wood.

Most animals seem better able to withstand extremes of weather than we can, but there are occasions when they welcome shelter from wind and rain or excessive sun. A shelter open on the side away from the prevailing wind allows animals to get some protection without you having to open doors or drive them in.

This shelter is intended for smaller animals, not for horses and cows (below). It is also a suitable size for you to use with chairs and loungers in your yard.

Shelter

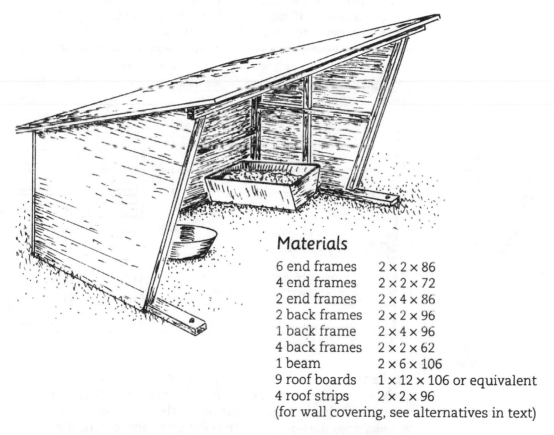

Materials

6 end frames	2 × 2 × 86
4 end frames	2 × 2 × 72
2 end frames	2 × 4 × 86
2 back frames	2 × 2 × 96
1 back frame	2 × 4 × 96
4 back frames	2 × 2 × 62
1 beam	2 × 6 × 106
9 roof boards	1 × 12 × 106 or equivalent
4 roof strips	2 × 2 × 96

(for wall covering, see alternatives in text)

Construction is sectional, with the walls framed and boarded. Covering could be shiplap boards, plain boards, old house siding or plywood. Most of the framing is 2-inch-square section, but 2-inch-by-4-inch pieces at the bottom give width for fixing to the ground. To provide resistance to movement, drive spikes through holes in these base pieces. Many details are the same as for the previous project, so you should examine the appropriate drawings.

Suggested sizes are for a shelter covering a floor 7 feet by 8 feet, with a height of 7 feet. You could modify these sizes, but do not make the shelter very much larger without increasing sections of wood. If the shelter will have to contend with snow for long periods, you might make the roof steeper.

Make a pair of ends (below). Only one intermediate rail is shown each way. If you use 1-inch boards for covering, they also will provide some strength, so these rails should be enough. However, for a light covering, you might want to arrange two rails each way. Use any of the frame joints suggested for the shed (see pages 126 and 127), except for the special corners.

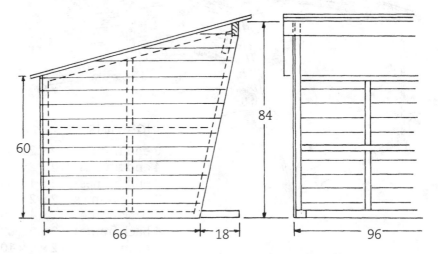

At the top front corner, leave space for the front 2-inch-by-6-inch beam. Inside, nail or screw a block to the upright and joint it to the top frame (top of next page). Use 2-inch-by-4-inch wood across the bottom, with the 2-inch face toward the covering and extending 18 inches forward for stability.

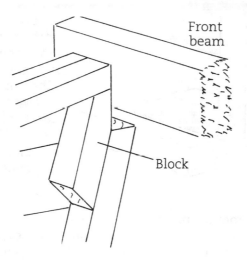

Front beam

Block

Check squareness, and make sure the opposite frames match as a pair. Then cover them all over, trimming edges level all around.

Make the back with its height to match the rear edges of the ends.

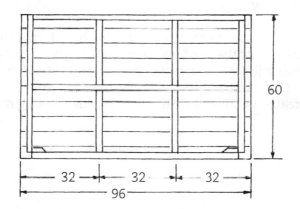

60

32

32

32

96

Corners of the shed have to be made with the back covering overlapping the ends, so arrange the framing far enough back (at right). Allow for the 4-inch-wide pieces at the bottom edges.

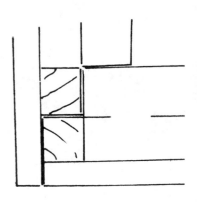

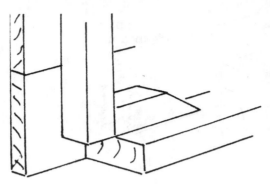

Cut back the bottom strip on the back and secure it to the upright with a block. Check squareness, and fit the covering level at the top and bottom, but extending enough at the ends.

Prepare the front beam (see top of page 133). The best fit is a beveled top edge, but you could still complete a satisfactory shelter with the edge left square. Make the edge long enough to extend over the ends as much as the roof—3 inches at each end will probably be enough.

Rear corners are joined with ⅜-inch carriage bolts. Drill the rear uprights on the ends at about 18-inch intervals. Then, when you assemble, put them in position and drill through the adjoining back frames. You can join the front beam with bolts in a similar way.

You could prefabricate the roof with wide boards in a similar way to the roof of the shed (see page 130), or you might choose to assemble and fix it on site. Put sufficient pieces across underneath to limit any tendency to warp. You could leave the roof untreated or cover it with tarred or other roofing material.

Mobile equipment

WHATEVER THE SIZE OF YOUR PROPERTY, you often will want to move loads heavier than you can carry easily. This means you need wheeled transport in most cases. If the property is extensive, you will probably have to settle for a tractor and wagon—which might be anything from a small combined tractor and mower to a full-size machine. For the larger transport, it would be best to buy a trailer or other carrying arrangement. For hauling purposes when you or an animal provide the power, though, you can make carts, barrows, and trolleys.

If you are concerned only with a garden, your carts can be simple and light, possibly with a single or close pair of wheels to negotiate narrow paths. On the other hand, if you need to move large quantities and weights over meadows or other larger areas, you need to think big.

In nearly all cases, it is best to buy wheels or reuse wheels from old vehicles. Even if you have a lathe to make them, wood wheels are rarely satisfactory and do not last long. For movement on hard surfaces the wheels can have narrow treads, but on soft ground, particularly if it is wet, your progress will be easier with treads as broad as possible. You could have inflated tires, but these require regular attention. Most loads do not need the cushioning of inflated tires, so wheels with solid rims or solid rubber tires are usually most suitable.

Wheels can attach to axles in various ways. Most fit on steel rods. If you have to make your own attachments, put a washer on each side of the wheel and drill the axle to take a cotter pin, shown at the top of next page.

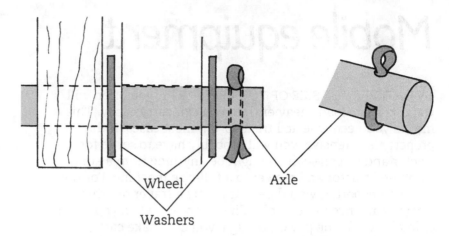

Wheel

Axle

Washers

Sack truck

Bags of feed, compost, fertilizer, and other powders or granules often come in bags or sacks that are heavier than you will want to carry very far. The old-time miller used a two-wheeled truck that could be positioned under a standing sack and tilted to move it about. This sack truck is a modified version that you can pack flat in your shed or garage and take out when needed to move bags or other loads over reasonably hard surfaces .

Materials

2 sides	1 × 2 × 44
4 rails	1 × 2 × 16
2 ends	1 × 2 × 16
3 end rails	¾ × 3 × 20

FEED

The truck is best made from hardwood; if you use softwood, increase wood widths slightly. Get your wheels and axle first. A wheel diameter of 5 inches is suitable. The drawing (below) shows a sack truck of a convenient length for handling, but if you anticipate hauling only small loads, you might shorten it slightly. The end fits outside the truck sides and will fold down for storage.

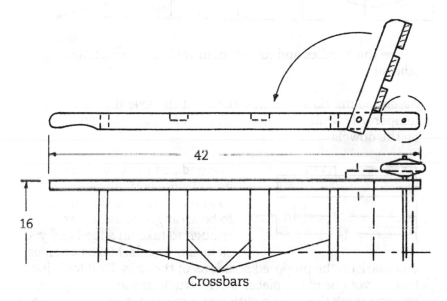

Crossbars

First, mark out a pair of sides (below). (Don't shape the handles until joints have been prepared.) The four crossbars could be tenoned into the sides, but dowels are suggested here.

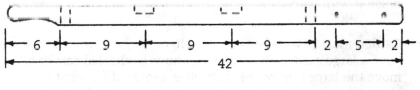

Cut four crossbars to the same length. Mark and drill for two ⅜-inch dowels at each position. They can go through the sides. Drill for the axle and round the corners at the end.

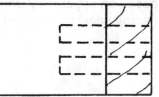

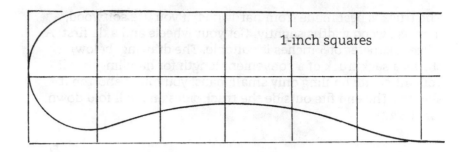

1-inch squares

Shape the handles and round them well for a comfortable grip (above).

Assemble the sides and crossbars. Put the axle through temporarily while you check squareness. Use waterproof glue on the dowels.

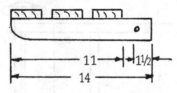

The end has to fit outside the main frame with just enough clearance to fold down, and it has to be arranged to swing far enough to take on a load and yet clear the wheels. Make two sides, and mark on the proposed positions of the rails. Drill for ¼-inch bolts. Pivot one of the pieces on the truck side and swing it so you can mark the exact position of a rail to act as a stop. Glue and screw the rails in place.

If you have used a good hardwood, the sack truck will look best if varnished. Otherwise, you might want to leave it untreated or finish it with paint.

Garden tool carrier

Garden tools have to be taken to where they are needed. If you have a large garden, it is helpful to have a wheeled carrier to move the large number of tools often required for what starts out as an apparently simple task. This garden tool carrier (facing page) is a tapered box.

Materials

2 box sides	15 × 60 × ½ plywood
1 box end	15 × 15 × ½ plywood
1 box end	15 × 21 × ½ plywood
1 bottom	21 × 57 × ½ plywood
1 top	24 × 62 × ½ plywood
2 shafts	1 × 3 × 9
2 side frames	1 × 2 × 62
6 side frames	1 × 2 × 12
2 end frames	1 × 2 × 16
2 end frames	1 × 2 × 13
2 end frames	1 × 2 × 21
2 end frames	1 × 2 × 19
2 bottom frames	1 × 2 × 60
1 bottom frame	1 × 2 × 20
1 bottom frame	1 × 2 × 14
2 lid frames	1 × 2 × 60
1 lid frame	1 × 2 × 20
1 lid frame	1 × 2 × 14

It can be moved on two close wheels and is a size to take tools as well as bags, pots, plants, and other items. This carrier can be fitted with a lid, which will protect the contents from rain if you leave the loaded carrier outside. With the lid on, you have a seat if you want to rest from your labors or just admire your work.

The box is made from ½-inch exterior grade plywood, framed on the outside, so there are no obstructions inside. Wheels 12 inches in diameter are suggested. The carrier is shown with a box 5 feet long (below), but you should measure the longest tool you want to transport and adjust the size if necessary. Although hardwood framing will make the strongest carrier, softwood is lighter. You could compromise with hardwood for the long shafts and softwood elsewhere.

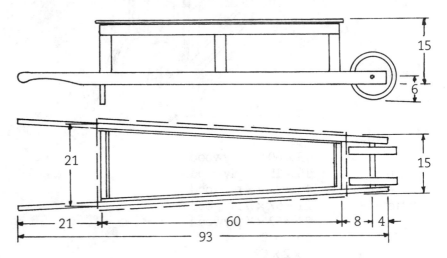

Get your wheels and axle first, since their size will affect some other sizes. The wheels and axle need clearance, and the legs must lift the other end to suit the wheels.

The pair of opposite sides are the key parts, so make them first (below). If you use waterproof glue between the plywood and framing, as well as plenty of nails or screws, you will not need to cut joints between frame parts.

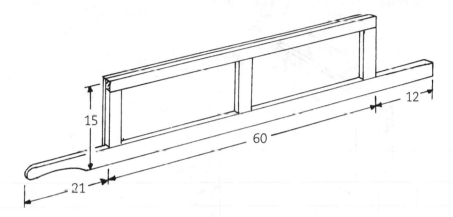

Shape the handles and well round them for comfortable grips (below).

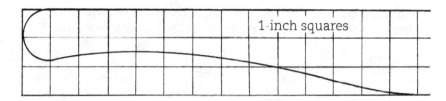

1-inch squares

The two ends fit between the sides, and the bottom goes inside them for greatest strength.

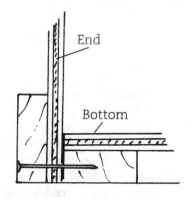

End

Bottom

The front is a framed square piece of plywood (below to the left). The back is similarly framed, but you have to take the uprights down to form legs (below to the right). Their length depends on how high the wheels lift the other end, and they should lift to that height or a little more.

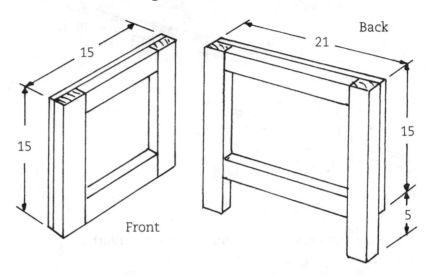

Although the probable sizes of the bottom are shown (below), check these against other parts to make the bottom a close fit.

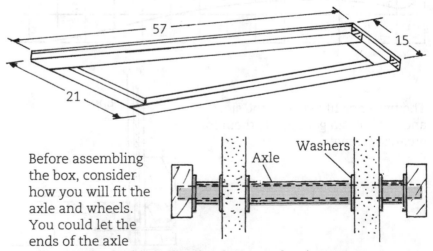

Before assembling the box, consider how you will fit the axle and wheels. You could let the ends of the axle into the wood. This is the simplest way, but it means you cannot remove the axle after assembly. If you think you might

142 *Outdoor Projects for the Country Home*

need to remove the axle and wheels later, drill through the wood, then cover the ends of the axle after assembly with wood or sheet-metal pads screwed on. Then you can remove the pads and drive the axle out later, if necessary.

Wheels far apart are steadier to push, but close wheels will follow narrower paths. You will have to compromise. Maintain wheel spacing with washers and metal tubes on the axle. The tubes do not have to be a close fit on the axle, and they should allow ample clearance for the wheels to rotate.

Assemble the box parts to each other with glue and nails or screws. Even if you use nails elsewhere, you might consider using long screws near the top corners, where most loads can be expected to come. You can put sheet metal covers around these corners. Fit the axles and wheels at the same time you join the wood parts.

A lift-off lid is suggested. This allows good access to the inside and it makes a good seat top. In addition, you might find uses for it on the ground, for kneeling or sorting plants, perhaps.

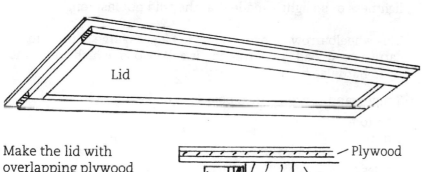

Lid

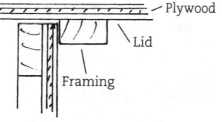

Make the lid with overlapping plywood and framing to fit easily inside.

Plywood

Lid

Framing

You could leave the carrier untreated, but it would be better treated with preservative or painted. A contrasting color, such as red, helps you to find the carrier amongst green foliage. A lighter color inside shows up the contents and encourages you to keep it clean.

Wheelbarrow

The traditional wheelbarrow has been developed over centuries on both sides of the Atlantic. The box to contain the load is tapered both ways for easy loading and unloading. The single wheel of good width and diameter will follow the narrowest path, while your arms provide push and the load remains steady, supported as it is in the triangle between your extended arms and the wheel. When it comes to tipping the load you can upend the barrow and everything goes out over the wheel end. A wheelbarrow is a piece of mobile equipment you can use in your yard or garden or on property of any size. It can do a variety of jobs, ranging from moving garden soil to mucking out animals or carrying their food.

Some traditional wheelbarrows were massively constructed, so they were heavy to move even without their load. At the other extreme have been barrows kept too small for the sake of lightness or so lightly made that they did not last long.

This wheelbarrow (shown on facing page) is large enough to carry a good load . Construction is solid wood, which will stand up to hard use better than plywood.

Materials

Tongue-and-groove 1-inch boards to make:

1 bottom	20 × 20
1 front	15 × 25
1 back	9 × 25
2 sides	15 × 33
2 shafts	2 × 2 × 52
2 crosspieces	2 × 2 × 20
2 legs	2 × 2 × 16
2 brackets	1 × 6 × 11

The box is made of 1-inch tongue-and-groove softwood boards about 6 inches wide (shown on page 146). The shafts and legs could also be softwood, but they would be better made of a straight-grained hardwood. Assembly should be with waterproof glue and screws. Where box parts overlap you could use 12-gauge-by-2½-inch or 3-inch screws at 3-inch to 4-inch intervals. Where screws will have their threaded parts in end grain, drill for ¾-inch dowels, so threads will pull into crosswise grain.

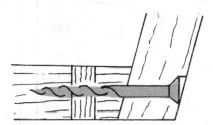

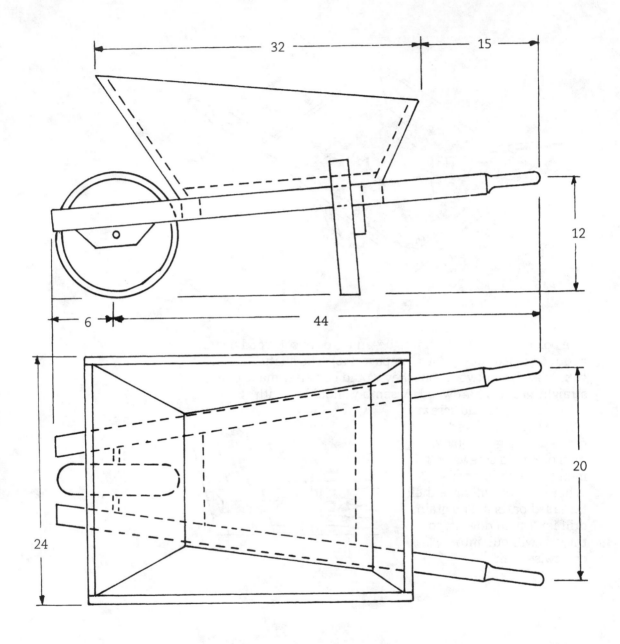

146 Outdoor Projects for the Country Home

The box has compound angles, but they need not present much of a problem if the parts are dealt with step by step. Draw an outline side view with the ends at 60° to the base (below). This will show you the angles at the top edges of the ends.

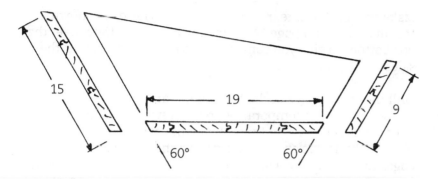

Make the bottom with boards crosswise. Use waterproof glue in the tongue-and-groove joints, then treat the bottom as a single piece when marking out and shaping. Leave the sides square at present, but bevel front and rear edges at 60° to take the ends.

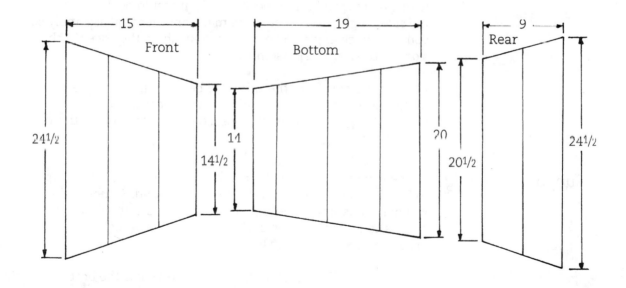

Sides and ends are shown with straight top edges. If you want, you could follow tradition and curve them up about 2 inches at their centers. This might look better, but it does not improve usefulness.

Make the front and rear in a similar way. These are shown in the illustration on page 147, ½ inch wider where they meet the box bottom to give you some wood to bevel when you fit the sides.

Drill the lower edges of the front and rear for screws. Join them to the box bottom temporarily—one screw near each end of a joint should be enough. From this temporary assembly, you have to obtain the shape of a side and the angles to make the edges to meet it. Use a spare piece of hardboard or plywood to form a template, and use it against the edges of the assembled parts to draw the required outline. With the template in position, note the angles you will have to plane the edges of the box front, rear, and bottom.

Unscrew the pieces and prepare their edges. Make up the sides with glued tongue-and-groove boards. It would be wise to cut the sides slightly too large, then make another trial assembly so you can check angles. You can leave finishing the edges of the sides until after final assembly.

All of the screws from the sides will be going into end grain, so fit dowels across at each position. The top corners can be expected to get the greatest loads, so put the top two or three screws closer together.

Support assembly

A wheel about 12 inches diameter is suggested. It could be up to 3 inches wide to resist sinking in soft ground. A rubber tire will make pushing easier on a hard surface, but it will be no better than a hard rim on soft ground. Such a wheel will probably need a ⅝-inch axle.

For the supporting parts of the wheelbarrow, use the bottom of the box as a guide. The two shafts should be about 1 inch in from its edges. The exact distance is not very important and it does not matter if the shafts are not exactly parallel edges, but get their sizes and positions by making a temporary assembly on the inverted box.

Ensure that there is ample space for the wheel and that those ends of the wood reach to the limit of the wheel or a little further. Then, when you tip the barrow near upright, it is the wood that takes the load. At the other end, arrange the grips about 20 inches apart. Mark on the box where the shafts come, and mark on shafts where the ends of the box come.

Make crosspieces to fit between the shafts, level with the ends of the box. Prepare mortises and tenons for these joints (shown at right). Glue and screw on blocks for the axle (shown at far right). You could mark and drill undersize pilot holes to locate the axle position, but leave drilling full-size until after assembly so you can get the slightly skew holes in line.

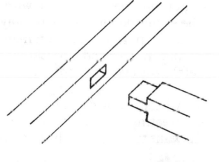
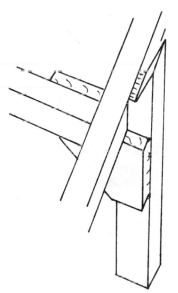

The grips are round and should not be more than 1½ inches diameter. Start by reducing 7 inches of the end to 1½ inches square, then take off corners to make it octagonal. Follow by removing these angles and, finally, round by sanding. Aim for a good finish, or you will soon suffer from sore hands!

Assemble the shafts and crosspieces. See that they are symmetrical by testing under the box. The legs have to be strongly supported to allow for awkward strains, as when scuffing along the ground. The legs come forward of the rear crosspiece, with space for supporting brackets.

Final assembly

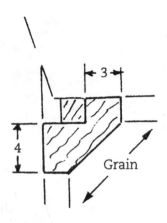

Grain

Screw the box in place on the framework, using similar screws to those used for assembling the box, spaced at 6-inch intervals all around. Allow for brackets 1 inch thick, and mark where the legs will come. Each leg can notch ½ inch under the shaft, then be bevelled to project a short distance up the box side (shown at far left).

Cut the brackets with the grain diagonal for greatest strength. Bolt each leg to its shaft with a central 1½-inch bolt. Glue and screw on the brackets, and screw where the top of each leg projects up the box side.

Center the wheel on its axle with washers and a piece of metal tube each side, similar to the way shown for twin wheels at the bottom of page 142. Friction might be all that is needed to hold the axle in the wood blocks, but you could put wood or sheet metal pads over the ends.

The wheelbarrow could be finished with preservative or paint. Any treatment inside will soon be worn away, but you probably will want to start with the barrow looking smart.

Sledge

Not every load you want to haul across your property needs wheels. One problem with wheeled transport is the height of the platform above the ground. Many loads are difficult to lift that high. If you want to move a large shelter in one piece, the less it has to be lifted from the ground, the better. If you are gathering bales of hay or heavy logs, you do not want to lift them far. A simple sledge allows you to drag a load at only a few inches above the ground behind a tractor or horse.

You can make a sledge from salvaged materials. This sledge (shown at top of next page) is a specimen with suggested sizes for parts and overall measurements, but you could adapt the sizes to suit wood that you have.

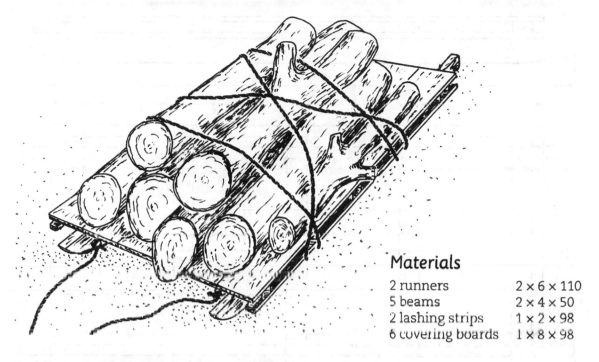

In this example, there is a platform 48 inches by 96 inches on runners 108 inches long. There are arrangements for tying down a load at the sides and towing arrangements are provided at both ends (as it is often less trouble to reverse a tow than to turn the sledge around).

First, assemble your materials. Arrange the platform to extend 4 inches beyond the runners at each side (shown on page 152). You might have to vary the total width to suit available covering boards. In the example, the six boards are 8 inches wide.

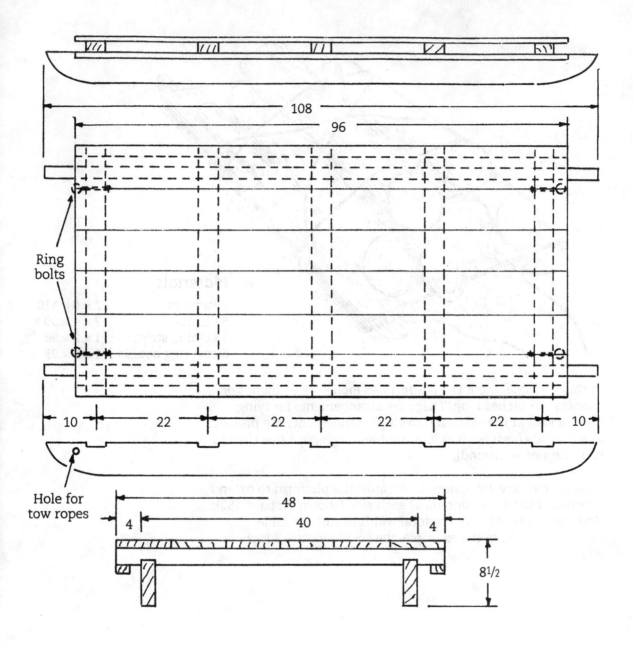

108

96

Ring
bolts

10   22   22   22   22   10

Hole for
tow ropes

48

4   40   4

8 1/2

Make the two runners with matching curves at the ends
(below). Notch ½ inch deep at each beam position, and round
the working edges of the runners for easy moving and to reduce
the risk of splintering.

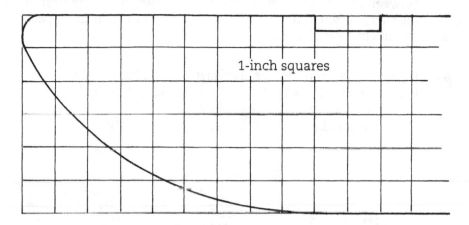

1-inch squares

Cut the beams all the same length, and securely nail them in
the notches in the runners. Check squareness. Nail on lashing
strips under the ends of the beams, letting their ends project
2 inches.

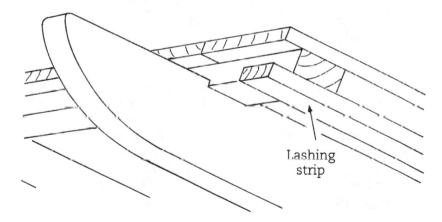

Lashing
strip

Drill near the corners of the end beams for ½-inch-diameter
ring bolts. A cheaper alternative is to drill the runners to take
tow ropes (shown on facing page). In any case, you need a high
pull to prevent the sledge from digging in.

Cover the top with 1-inch boards, level at the sides and extending 2 inches past the beams at the ends.

When you tow, make sure the rope shares the strain equally between the attachment points. A short strop keeps the front of the sledge lifted, but a longer strop puts less load on the rope and might be easier to steer.

Light trailer

If you have a small ride-on mower/tractor, a light trailer will increase its usefulness. It would be unwise to overload it, but this trailer (below) is not heavy in itself and, even with a full load, it should be easy to pull about your property.

Materials

2 box sides	14 × 50 × ¾ plywood	2 box edges	1 × 2 × 36
1 box front	12 × 36 × ¾ plywood	2 box brackets	2 × 4 × 14
1 box door	12 × 36 × ¾ plywood	1 box beam	2 × 4 × 38
1 box bottom	36 × 48 × ¾ plywood	3 box beams	2 × 4 × 48
2 box joints	2 × 2 × 14	2 chassis sides	2 × 4 × 84
1 box joint	2 × 2 × 36	2 axle beams	2 × 4 × 40
2 box edges	1 × 2 × 52	2 axle blocks	2 × 4 × 14
4 door guides	1 × 1 × 14		

The suggested sizes (next page) show a box 3 feet by 4 feet by 1 foot. With wheels 14 inches diameter, the inside of the box is 15 inches above the ground when the trailer is level. The box is arranged 24 inches from the towing hitch. Because methods of

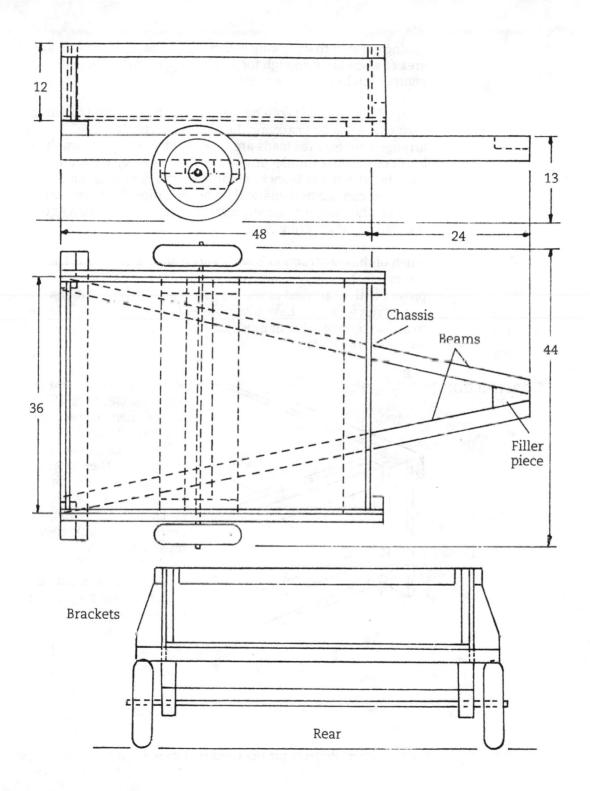

12

13

48   24

Chassis

Beams

44

36

Filler
piece

Brackets

Rear

joining a trailer to its towing vehicle vary, the design shows an area of wood large enough for a bolt-on plate with a hole or another hitching arrangement.

The pulling strain is taken by a V-shaped chassis going to the back of the box and carrying the axle supports. This arrangement ensures loads are integrated, so the parts won't break or pull apart under strain. For the example, it is assumed that the wheels are 14 inches diameter on a ¾-inch-diameter axle. You can use pneumatic tires or solid rims. If you use other sizes of wheels, you must allow for them altering the height of the trailer and affecting its angle when towed.

Much of the construction is with 2-inch-by-4-inch wood. The box is ¾-inch exterior-grade plywood. This is an excellent project to use salvaged or reused materials. Slight variations in size to suit what you have available will not matter. It will help to use waterproof glue in most joints, but you can do a lot with plenty of long nails.

Construction

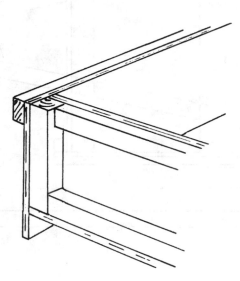

Start by making a pair of box sides (see page 155). Extend them at the front to take in 2-inch joint stiffeners, as shown. At the bottom, they extend 2 inches over the side beams and will be notched over the rear beam. At the back, they finish level with the beam. Make the front to fit between them with a 2-inch-square strip along its lower edge.

Make the front beam to fit between the sides, and make the rear beam to extend enough to take supports. Make two lengthwise beams to fit between the crosswise beams. You can notch them together at the back. Either do the same at the front, or halve the beams together.

At the back of the box there is a lift-off door that drops between guides (below left). Strengthen the top edges of the box with 1-inch-by-2-inch strips. Support the rear ends of the sides with brackets (below right), which fit under the top edge pieces. Mortise-and-tenon joints, glued and screwed, are advisable here; some loads you carry might put considerable outward thrust on the sides.

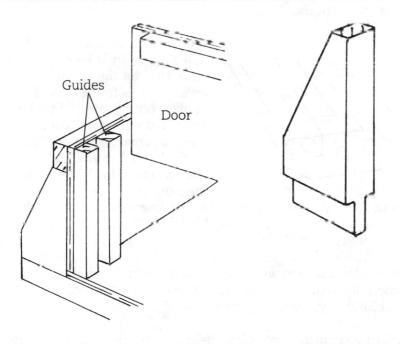

Guides

Door

Cut a plywood bottom and assemble the box on its beams. Trim the edges level, and round the corners.

Next, invert the box and make a trial fitting with the wood that will make the chassis. These parts are shown extending from the rear corners of the beams under the box to meet with a filler piece at the towing end (see page 155). You might need to alter this to suit your towing arrangements. The two pieces must match and assemble symmetrically or your trailer will not tow straight. Join the chassis strips together and to the beams. Bolts through will be better than nails or screws.

The axle-supporting frame is best made as a unit; then the wheels and axle attached before the whole assembly is attached to the chassis strips. With most wheels, there should be ample clearance if you make the frame length the same as the width of the box, but you can vary this if you want a wider spread of wheels.

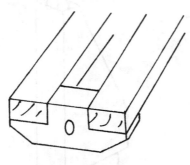 Cut two beams to length and make blocks to fit between their ends. Drill for the axle and assemble this framework. Try it in place on the inverted trailer. Your load will travel best if there is some downward thrust on the hitch, but you do not want so much load there that the front of the trailer is difficult to lift. If you arrange the axle line 3 inches behind the center of the box, balance should be right. Mark where the parts meet.

Mount the axle and wheels to the wood parts, then attach the assembly to the chassis members, preferably with bolts. Be careful that you work squarely.

When you finish by painting, make sure the plywood edges are sealed well enough to prevent entry of water.

Large buildings

MAKING A LARGE SHELTER FOR HORSES OR COWS, a barn to hold produce, or a roofed area for cars or machinery need not be more difficult to build than a smaller project. Of course, certain problems are particular to dealing with large projects. You will be dealing with heavy pieces of wood, so you will need assistance at some stages. With smaller projects, you might have tossed a piece of wood around on the bench to work on different parts of it; with larger ones, you need to plan ahead so you don't end up moving heavy lumber more than is necessary. (If you can fell your own trees, you can plan a building around your available timber.)

The technique of cutting large joints is no different from cutting small ones, but you need the equipment for making large cuts and drilling large holes. You also will be faced with the necessity of doing more work at the site. You probably won't be able to prefabricate much in the comfort of your shop, and you probably won't be able to use electrically powered tools, unless you have a generator. A cordless drill will be useful.

In planning your large-building project, you should consider the effect of wind, particularly in an exposed position. Large animals could also have devastating effects on your project. Make sure all parts of the building are securely held down. If wind cannot lift the building off the ground, it might still be able to push it out of shape—so could a cow running amok! Properly jointed wood of adequate size and strength will do much to resist wind pressure, but the design of the building has an effect, too.

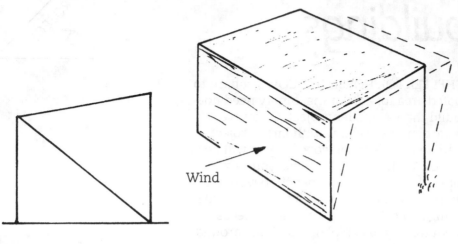

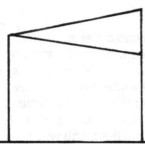

Wind

If you board one side of a shelter, any wind against that might push it over. Diagonal struts (shown at the far left) would resist this because they would, in effect, triangulate the ends, and a triangle with rigid sides cannot be pushed out of shape.

If you need headroom at an end and the strut to the floor would be an obstruction, you can arrange a higher triangle, such as the one shown, or cross two of them, such as the shelter shown below. The method works in any direction.

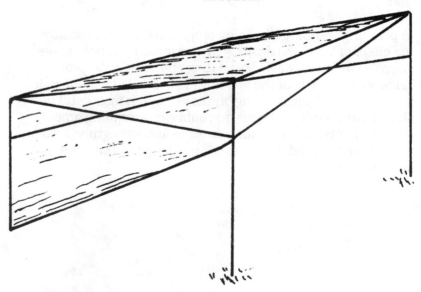

Closing the ends serves the same purpose. In effect, in regard to bracing, you have made an infinite number of triangles. Boards could move against each other under pressure, so the building might still distort slightly, but it would not collapse.

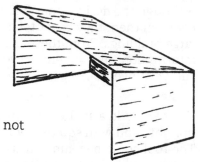

As far as possible, avoid a fully open side or end (below left). Some framing and boarding high up or framing all around will give stiffness (below right).

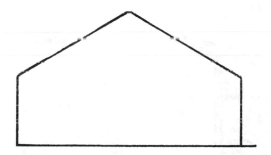 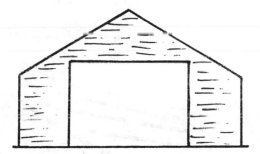

In a large building with a roof made of many metal or other sheets, which do not contribute enough to stiffening, you have to triangulate to hold shape against wind pressure. You can put wind bracing diagonally under purlins. Plywood on roof or walls provides its own triangulating. You cannot push a sheet of plywood out of shape.

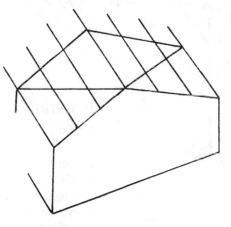

Although the designs that follow are self-contained projects, between them they cover techniques for constructing many large buildings. From these instructions, you should find information that will enable you to tackle other buildings to suit your needs.

Cattle shelter

You can build a shelter for animals with round poles as uprights and with squared wood for roof supports and framing. The roof could be plain boards, boards covered with roofing felt or other material, corrugated metal, or plastic sheets.

This shelter (below) is open all round, but you could close one or more walls. It is not excessively high, but there is headroom for you over most of the area.

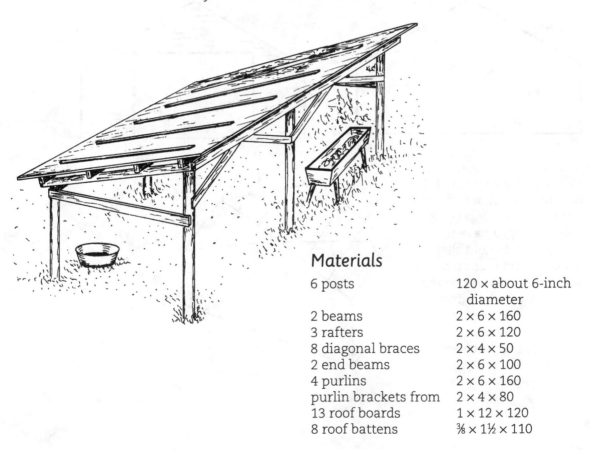

Materials

6 posts	120 × about 6-inch diameter
2 beams	2 × 6 × 160
3 rafters	2 × 6 × 120
8 diagonal braces	2 × 4 × 50
2 end beams	2 × 6 × 100
4 purlins	2 × 6 × 160
purlin brackets from	2 × 4 × 80
13 roof boards	1 × 12 × 120
8 roof battens	⅜ × 1½ × 110

The uprights should be poles about 6 inches diameter, but it would not matter if there are variations. Other parts are standard softwood sizes, but there are several places where you could vary details to use salvaged wood.

The shelter is shown covering about 8 feet by 12 feet, with six uprights. Although extreme accuracy is not important, your shelter should be built reasonably square for the sake of appearance.

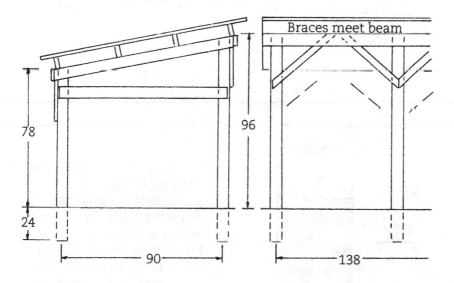

Set out positions of the uprights and their holes with pegs and cords, using the 3:4:5 method. In a triangle with the sides in those proportions, the angle between the short sides is 90°.

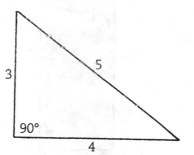

In this case, set out the 12-foot side, which is four units of 3 feet. Measure from its ends 9 feet (3 units) and 15 feet (5 units) to a point. If you take a cord from that point to the end of the line, it will be square to the base. Measure from these lines to mark the positions of the post poles.

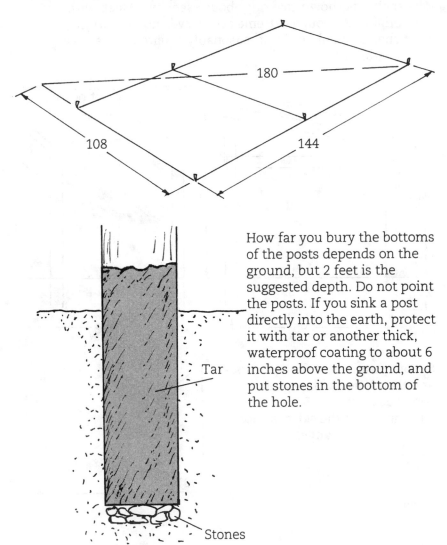

How far you bury the bottoms of the posts depends on the ground, but 2 feet is the suggested depth. Do not point the posts. If you sink a post directly into the earth, protect it with tar or another thick, waterproof coating to about 6 inches above the ground, and put stones in the bottom of the hole.

Another, stronger solution is to use concrete. Extend it a few inches around the post, and slope the top of the concrete to shed water.

As you erect the posts, check that they are upright, and brace them to each other with temporary strips nailed on to keep them in position. Sight across the assembly to see that the posts match. Leave them this way until the cement has set.

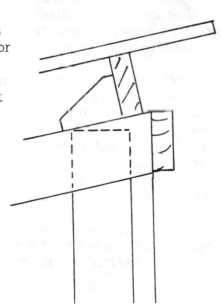

It would be unwise to prepare the joints in the posts or cut them to length before mounting them in the ground, as you are unlikely to get all the heights correct, particularly since the ground is probably not level.

Mark the heights of the posts at one end and cut notches for the rafters (shown at the far right). Cut away only enough for the rafter to bear on a flat surface large enough to take two ½-inch bolts. Make upright cuts at both ends of the rafter, 2 inches from the posts (right). The ends will take the lengthwise beams and the gap is for the diagonal braces.

Use this assembly as a guide when you fit rafters at the other two positions. Use a straight board and a spirit level to get heights the same crosswise, and sight across to see that slopes are the same. Fit the rafter either side of the middle posts, but have the end rafters outside the posts. Although bolts through are best for joining rafters to posts, you might get satisfactory results with long nails.

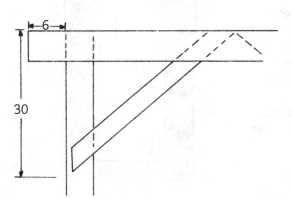

Fit lengthwise beams to the ends of the rafters, extending 6 inches each way. Join these to the posts with diagonal braces inside the beams and into shallow notches in the posts (see margin of page 165). The exact angles are not important, but arrange braces to meet on the beams.

Fit beams across the posts at both ends, nailed or bolted into shallow notches. You will now have a rigid structure ready for roofing. See that all joints are close and secure, and trim any ragged or rough edges or ends.

The roof is shown supported on four purlins, which extend the same amount as the beams. If you intend on using corrugated metal or plastic sheeting and there have to be overlapping sheets down the slope, arrange one purlin in a position to take nails driven through the overlapping sheets. Otherwise, for full-length sheets or boarding, you can space the purlins evenly. Nail brackets to the rafters, and nail the purlins to them. The brackets must be reversed for the lower purlin.

For a boarded roof, nail on wide boards to overhang about 6 inches at the back and front. If drips through the cracks will not matter, you can leave the roof without further treatment.

For a more weatherproof roof, cover the wood with tarred felt or other roofing material, held down with large-head nails. You could lay the covering lengthwise, starting at the lower edge and allowing a good overlap between rows. Another option is to lay the covering from high to low edges, still with broad overlaps held with plenty of large-head nails. Turn the material under at the edges, and nail there (top right). For the strongest joints, nail through thin battens (right). Light battens at about 18-inch intervals on the roof will hold the covering down and prevent it from lifting during high winds (below).

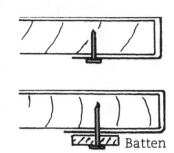

Batten

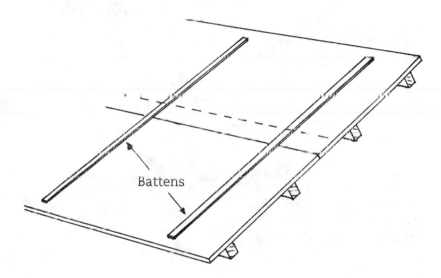

Battens

Finish the roof with tar or bitumastic paint. Leave the other woodwork untreated, or finish it with preservative or paint. If you have used unseasoned wood, leave it untreated for as much as two years so it dries out before you apply any finish.

Barn

Most people can use a large storage building on their property. You might call it a barn, but it could serve as a stable or many other purposes. This building, shown on page 168, covers 10 feet by 16 feet and is 10 feet high to the ridge. It has double doors at one end, with one door in two parts for inspection or ventilation. Two windows are provided at the other end.

Materials

Ends

9 frames	2 × 4 × 120
8 frames	2 × 4 × 96
5 frames	2 × 4 × 72
6 frames	2 × 4 × 24
brackets from	2 × 4 × 84

Sides

16 frames	2 × 4 × 96
4 fillers	1 × 2 × 96
2 fillers	1 × 1 × 96

Roof

2 ridge pieces	2 × 6 × 104
12 purlins	2 × 4 × 84
4 truss rafters	2 × 4 × 80
2 truss ties	2 × 4 × 72
brackets from	2 × 4 × 84
34 boards	1 × 12 × 84 or equivalent plywood
20 battens	½ × 1½ × 72
12 end fillers	1 × 2 × 30

Doors

7 ledgers	1 × 6 × 36
4 braces	1 × 6 × 42
8 sides	1 × 3 × 36
2 linings	1 × 5 × 80
1 lining	1 × 6 × 74
1 door top	1 × 1 × 74

Windows

4 linings	1 × 6 × 26
4 linings	1 × 7 × 26
8 strips	1 × 2 × 26
8 strips	1 × 1 × 26

Cladding

Shiplap boards   1-x-6 or equivalent siding or plywood

Construction is mainly with 2-inch-by-4-inch section framing and a wall covering of 1-inch shiplap boards. You have your choice of covering for the roof.

The method of construction used here would be suitable for buildings of many sizes. For a small building, you could reduce the sections of wood used for framing. You could put windows and doors in other positions. The instructions that follow are for sizes as drawn on the following page, but if you understand the methods of construction, you can adapt them to make a building to suit your needs.

The barn is sectional, so you can make parts elsewhere and assemble them on site. There are two ends, two pairs of side sections, and two roof trusses—all of which can be made as units, then brought together on site. Roofing is done when the other parts are in position. Although dimensions are given, extreme accuracy is not important. However, as you prepare sections, be sure that adjoining parts match when they are brought together. Make the door end first, then the other end with an identical outline, followed by the pair of sides to match heights of the ends, then trusses to match the tops of the ends.

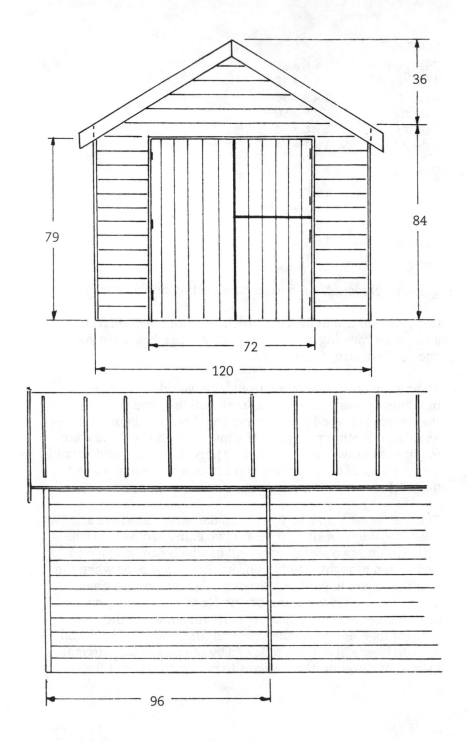

170 Outdoor Projects for the Country Home

All the framing at the door end has its 2-inch face toward the covering. You should find it satisfactory simply to nail most framing parts together. Use halving joints where pieces cross. For positive location, you can cut shallow grooves.

At the sides and door edges of the end, cut the covering boards level with the framing. You have to allow for the 4-inch depth of the purlins at the top.

Construction

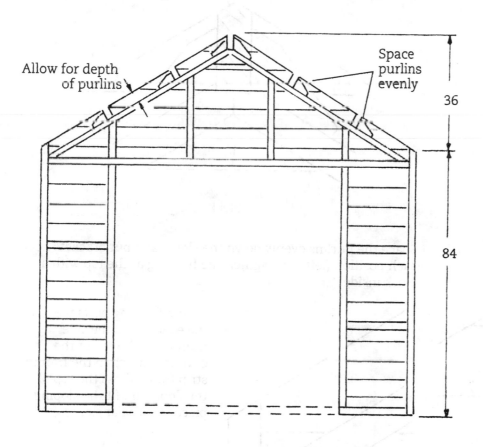

Allow for depth of purlins

Space purlins evenly

36

84

The covering goes to the outline of the end and is notched for the purlins and the ridge piece, but the framing is dropped 4 inches, and you need to allow for a 2-inch-by-6-inch ridge piece (shown below).

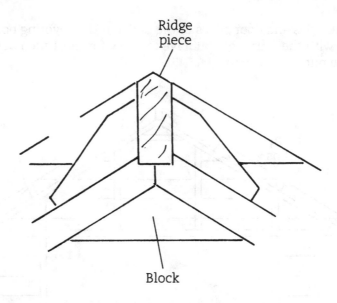

Ridge piece

Block

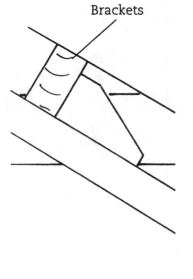

Brackets

Space the purlins evenly down the slope, and put brackets at each position (left). Strengthen the framing at the top with a block inside.

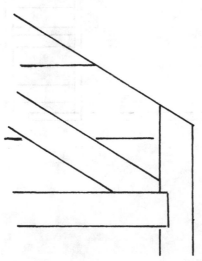

Where framing parts meet at the eaves, take the side framing to the top of the covering, notch in the framing strip from across the top of the door, and fit the sloping piece into the angle.

Build the end with the bottom part of the framing going across the doorway. You might want to keep this in the finished barn (it acts as a door stop), but if you do not want it, leave it in place to control the shape of the end, until after erection; then cut it off.

Make the opposite end (below) to the same outline, but arrange upright framing spaced evenly in the width and with horizontal framing across, so you can allow two window spaces.

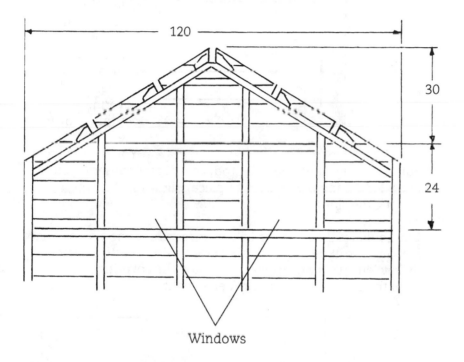

Windows

The window arrangement shown should admit enough daylight, and the position is high enough to be clear of most animals. You could alter the window design or include a small door. In some situations, you might prefer to move windows to a side. For a working area, it would be better to have windows just above bench height.

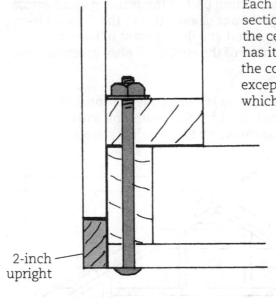

Each side is in two sections joined on site at the center. Framing all has its 2-inch face toward the covering boards, except the top pieces, which have the 4-inch way upright. You need two pairs of sides. When you assemble the building, the side framing butts against the end frame, but the covering continues over the end upright. You could take it out to the edge, but you will produce a neater corner if you allow for a 2-inch-wide upright piece. Allow for this when making the sides (left).

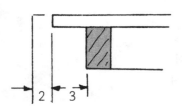

2-inch upright

You could let the covering boards meet where the side panels join, but it will be neater to allow for a 1-inch vertical strip (below left). This means you must stop the covering ½ inch from the edge of the framing (below right).

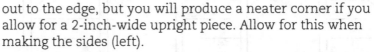

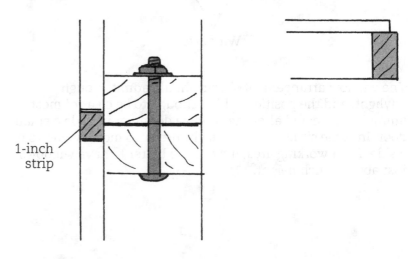

1-inch strip

Notch the upright frames over the top framing strip. You have to allow for the slope of the roof. For the best fit of the roof covering at the eaves, bevel the frame and the edge of the covering board. Other options are to leave the framing square and bevel only the covering board, or to partially bevel the frame as well as the covering board. However, neither of these alternatives gives such good bearing surfaces when you nail on the roof. Allow for the amount of beveling when you match the height of sides to the ends.

Notch

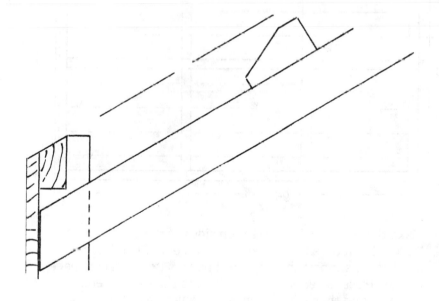

There are two roof trusses attached to the side uprights (below) so as to divide the length of the roof into three almost-equal parts.

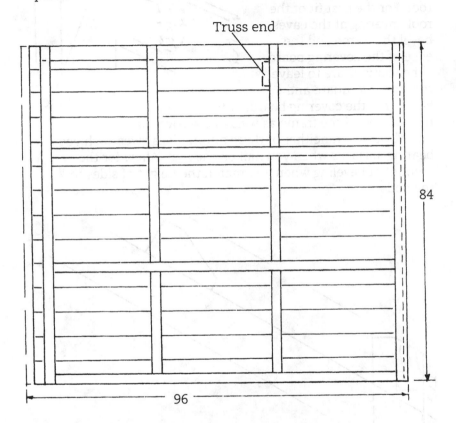

Truss end

84

96

Make the trusses with the 4-inch sides of the parts upright. Match the outline to the framing of an end, including the brackets to support the ridge and purlins (top of facing page). Cut the truss rafter ends level with the sides of the end framing, and they will fit inside the covering of the sides (bottom of page 175). Nail on the tie and the ridge cover to hold each truss in shape. Check that the trusses match each other and the ends.

This completes prefabricating of the main parts. You could make and fit the doors and windows now or leave them until after the building is erected. Instructions follow for erection, and the making of doors and windows comes last.

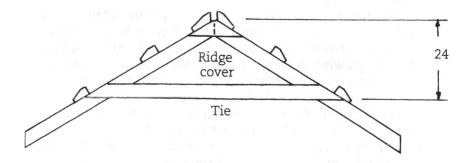

Ridge
cover

Tie

24

A building of this size is best erected on concrete. The broad bottom framing allows space for plenty of holding-down bolts. If you do not want concrete over the whole area, you could lay a base up to 2 feet wide all around, and bolt to that. Instead of concrete, you could let substantial balks of wood into the ground and spike to them. If you erect directly on the ground, it would be a good idea to drive in posts at the corners and at intervals along the walls, and secure the building to them. The weight of the building will do much to hold it in place, but it should also be securely held down. Whatever the method of mounting, make sure the walls will stand level.

Erection

Besides leveling where the walls will come, square the base, so you erect parts without twist. Corner joints can be nailed or you could use bolts. You should find it strong enough to nail at about 12-inch intervals, while bolts might be 18 inches apart. Use bolts throughout if you think you might eventually want to disassemble the barn. Nail or bolt where side sections meet. Fit the upright trim pieces at the corners and the centers of the sides. Put a temporary strip across the tops of the sides near the center of the building to keep the walls in line.

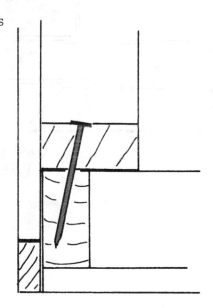

Position the trusses on their side frame uprights. Clamp them in place first, so you can adjust them. Check that they are in line with each other and with the ends by sighting along and trying lengthwise strips of wood between parts. Then nail or bolt the trusses in place, and remove the temporary strip.

You probably will not be able to get wood (for purlins or the ridge piece) that is as long as the barn and, if you can, the wood might not be straight. You can join the purlins over the trusses and the ridge at the center. All these parts should extend 4 inches over the ends of the building. Make a ridge joint at the center.

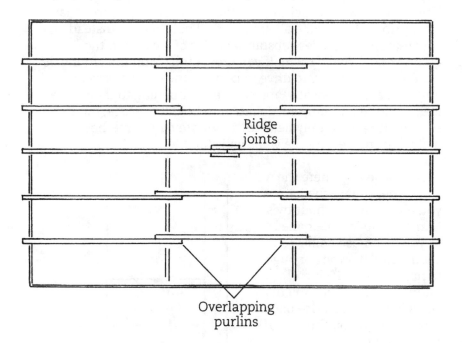

Ridge joints

Overlapping purlins

Nail or screw on joint covers at each side with their edges kept low enough to clear the roof boards or sheets.

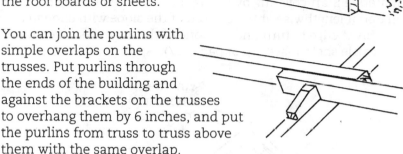

You can join the purlins with simple overlaps on the trusses. Put purlins through the ends of the building and against the brackets on the trusses to overhang them by 6 inches, and put the purlins from truss to truss above them with the same overlap.

Roof covering

You could use corrugated metal or plastic sheets to cover the roof. Arrange the sheets to meet on the ridge piece and overhang 6 inches at the eaves. If you need joints on the slope, arrange them to come over purlins (however, the length needed is 78 inches, and you should be able to buy sheets that length). Fit a matching covering strip along the ridge.

Nail ½-inch or ¾-inch plywood on the roof framing and cover it with tarred felt or other covering material. Instead of plywood, you can use wide boards at least ¾ inch thick. Whatever roof you use, it has to reach the ends of the purlins and overhang 6 inches at the eaves. You need to cut a reasonably close joint along the ridge, but it will be waterproofed by the covering material, anyway. If you use plywood, thicken its edge below the eaves with a ¾-inch-by-1½-inch strip (or larger), nailed below to give a stouter edge for nailing the felt or other covering material.

Plan your method of fitting the covering material so one piece can go over the ridge. Take off any roughness where the plywood or boards meet on the ridge, then nail on a strip of material. Start covering by laying the tarred felt or other material lengthwise at the bottom of the slope with enough at the eaves edge to turn under in one of the ways described for the cattle shelter (see top of page 167).

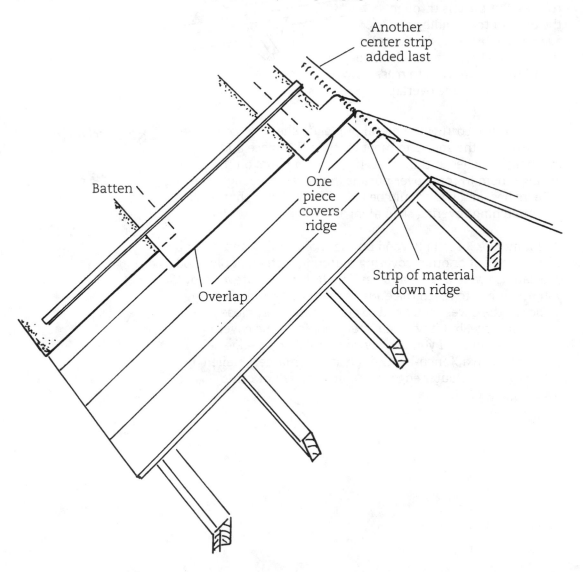

Another
center strip
added last

Batten

One
piece
covers
ridge

Strip of material
down ridge

Overlap

Leave enough at the ends for turning under. Nail this piece securely, then add the next with a good overlap. Do the same at the other side, then fit the piece that overhangs the ridge. A finishing touch is provided by a strip centrally.

Turn in at each end, and nail underneath and to the ends of the purlins and ridge piece. Cover the turn-in with 1-inch-by-2-inch strips between the purlins to give increased area for nailing on the bargeboards. These are plain boards meeting at the ridge and cut upright at their outer ends. Fit them so their top edges are ¼ inch above the finished roof level.

Strip between purlins

Further secure the roof covering with light battens (see facing page) from near the ridge to near the eaves. Space them at 18-inch intervals.

Line the door opening with strips that have their front edges level with the covering boards at the sides, so the doors can swing back without interference, but let the top piece project a little. Put a strip under the top to act as a door stop. You could put similar strips down the sides, for draft-proofing, but they are not essential.

Door stop

Door & window construction

The double doors are shown with one full-depth and the other divided 3 feet from the top. You could arrange them either way, or have both solid or both in two parts. Just be sure to allow enough clearance for the doors to swing easily and that there is enough space above the ground.

The framing suggested is 1 inch thick, but you might have offcuts from other parts of the building that you can use. The covering is upright and could be shiplap, tongue-and-groove, or plain boards. If you have to cut down boards to suit the width, have full-width boards at the outsides and any reduced-width boards inside, to get the maximum strength at the edges. Construction can be with nails or screws. Waterproof glue would increase strength.

Arrange the central ledger on the tall door level with the top of the other lower door. Include vertical strips at the edges between ledgers, and cut diagonal braces to slope upwards from the hinge side and to fit closely in the corners (below).

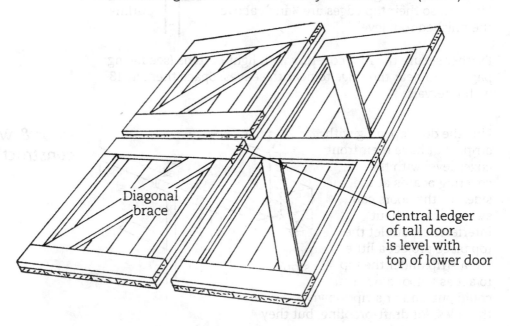

Diagonal brace

Central ledger of tall door is level with top of lower door

The doors are fairly heavy and need strong hinges. Use 4-inch or larger butt hinges let into the edges, or put T-hinges on the surface. Locate the hinges at ledger levels.

Arrange a bolt inside to fasten the two parts of the divided door together. Put bolts top and bottom inside the long door, into a hole in the top framing and into the bottom framing or a block let into the floor. Provide a lock or latch that allows you to open the divided door without the other, and provide handles for both parts.

Line the window openings, preferably with pieces projecting outwards. Have the side pieces ½ inch out from the surface of the cladding. The bottom part can be wider and beveled to form a sill. The top part should be made in a similar way, but it need not project as much. Put strips round to come behind the glass. After the building has been erected, fit the glass and secure it with more strips. So you will be able to remove the strips if you ever have to replace the glass, use just a few nails that can be prized out, or attach the outer strips with screws.

Strips for glass

Bevel to form sill

Final touches

You can use the barn as it is, but lining it completely or partially provides protection and insulation. Plywood nailed to wall framing could come 4 feet high to take knocks from inside and present a smooth surface that could be an advantage in storage or cleaning.

Tar the roof or coat it with bitumastic paint. The walls could be treated with preservative, but paint might look better, particularly if you have mixed salvaged and new wood in construction. The bargeboards might look better in a contrasting color.

Workshop

If you expect to do much maintenance or other work about your property, you will soon feel the need for a special place where you can keep a bench, tools, and other equipment, and where you can work in comfort at any time of the year. You might manage in part of a building used mainly for other purposes, but a shop devoted only to wood and metal work is much better.

This workshop (below) is 8 feet by 12 feet, with standing headroom and windows along one side. It is designed to make good use of plywood (2 sheets by 3 sheets). Plywood contributes considerable strength. With plywood inside and out there is an air gap to provide insulation. If you want to increase this, you could pack the spaces with insulating plastic foam. The light framing takes account of the strength of two skins of plywood. If you decide to clad with boards or omit the inside panels, you should increase the sections of wood used for framing to allow for the reduction in skin strength.

Materials

Covering

20 wall sheets	48 × 96 × ½ plywood
5 roof sheets	48 × 96 × ¾ plywood
4 floor sheets	48 × 96 × ¾ plywood

End framing

17 pieces	$1\frac{1}{2} \times 1\frac{1}{2} \times 98$
14 pieces	$1\frac{1}{2} \times 1\frac{1}{2} \times 24$
2 door borders	$\frac{3}{4} \times 3 \times 78$
1 door border	$\frac{3}{4} \times 3\frac{1}{2} \times 76$
1 door border	$\frac{3}{4} \times 3\frac{1}{2} \times 38$
2 corner covers	$\frac{3}{4} \times 3 \times 80$
2 corner covers	$\frac{3}{4} \times 3 \times 98$

Front and rear framing

10 pieces	$1\frac{1}{2} \times 1\frac{1}{2} \times 144$
2 pieces	$1\frac{1}{2} \times 1\frac{1}{2} \times 98$
7 pieces	$1\frac{1}{2} \times 1\frac{1}{2} \times 80$
5 pieces	$1\frac{1}{2} \times 1\frac{1}{2} \times 48$
8 pieces	$1\frac{1}{2} \times 1\frac{1}{2} \times 32$
2 window borders	$\frac{3}{4} \times 3 \times 80$
2 window borders	$\frac{3}{4} \times 3 \times 38$
6 window linings	$\frac{3}{4} \times 4\frac{1}{2} \times 32$
4 window linings	$\frac{3}{4} \times 5\frac{1}{2} \times 20$
2 window linings	$\frac{3}{4} \times 5\frac{1}{2} \times 38$
2 joint covers	$\frac{3}{4} \times 3 \times 98$
2 joint covers	$\frac{3}{4} \times 3 \times 48$
2 joint covers	$\frac{3}{4} \times 3 \times 18$

Roof framing

3 rafters	$2 \times 3 \times 100$
6 rafter supports	$2 \times 3 \times 12$
8 battens	$\frac{1}{2} \times 1\frac{1}{2} \times 96$

Door framing

2 sides	$1\frac{1}{2} \times 1\frac{1}{2} \times 78$
6 crossbars	$1\frac{1}{2} \times 1\frac{1}{2} \times 36$
2 sides	$\frac{1}{2} \times 2\frac{1}{2} \times 80$
2 ends	$\frac{1}{2} \times 2\frac{1}{2} \times 38$

Windows

6 borders	$1 \times 2 \times 32$
4 borders	$1 \times 2 \times 20$
2 borders	$1 \times 2 \times 38$
4 fixed window strips	$1 \times 1 \times 32$
1 fixed window strip	$1 \times 1 \times 20$
2 window frames	$1\frac{1}{2} \times 1\frac{1}{2} \times 38$
2 window frames	$1\frac{1}{2} \times 1\frac{1}{2} \times 32$

Sizes (shown below) allow for using standard 8-foot-by-4-foot plywood sheets with the minimum of cutting. If you alter sizes, allow for sheet sizes and try to have joints vertical as far as possible. In the design shown, you can place the door at either or both ends and arrange windows differently. Windows are described as one opening pane between two fixed ones.

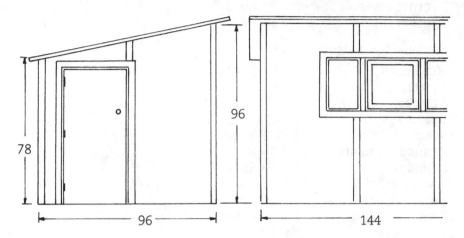

Main construction

Start with the door end (shown on facing page). Put two sheets of plywood against each other, and mark the slope of the roof. The edge of one sheet is the edge of the door. Mark and cut the door opening in the other sheet, and then cut the roof slope. You might find it wisest to cut a little way outside the lines, so you can trim edges to the framing after it has been fitted.

Mark on the plywood where the internal framing parts will come, and drill through a few nail holes to serve as guides when nailing from the other side. Use waterproof glue and plenty of nails. It should be sufficient to let most ends of framing butt against adjoining pieces, but you will have to cut halving joints where horizontal pieces cross uprights. Notch the end of the doorhead into the upright.

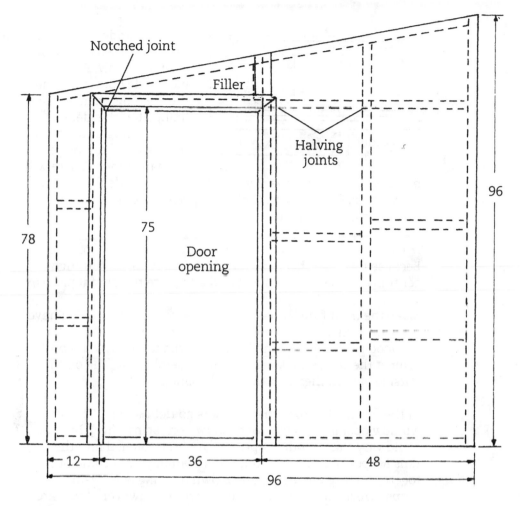

Notched joint

Filler

Halving joints

78

75

Door opening

96

12 — 36 — 48

96

Top and bottom strips and the doorhead go across. All uprights are full-length. Other parts fill in and need not be in line. Put a filler at the top to support the narrow pieces of plywood.

When all this assembly is completed, cut the plywood for the other surface to match, and glue and nail it on. Be careful to keep edges square when you trim plywood to the framing.

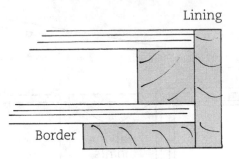

Lining

Border

The door opening has to be lined, and you can do this now or leave it until after assembly. Put a 3-inch-wide border around the opening, then add a lining at each side. A similar lining at the top of the doorway can project outward 1 inch. There will be a door stop, but leave that until you have made the door and know its exact thickness. Cover the plywood joint above the door with a 3-inch strip.

Make the opposite end to match the outline of the door end. Because it will be sheeted over, though, put an extra upright centrally on the shorter sheet and add more horizontal pieces.

Make the front from three upright sheets of plywood. You have to allow 2½ inches for the joints to the ends, where the outer plywood goes over and the frame and the inner plywood butt against the shed end. Mark out and assemble framing on the outside panels; then add the inside panels.

In the front, all horizontal members go right across. The total window opening is 6 feet long (shown on facing page), but you could vary this. Window uprights are best notched into their rails for positive location, but other framing parts could butt together. The panel edges are shown meeting over 1½-inch strips, which should be a sufficient width. However, if you are using narrower wood for framing, you should substitute wider pieces for strength at the joints.

See that the height of the front matches where it meets the ends. For the best fit of the roof, bevel the top frame strip and plywood. With all frame strips attached to the outside plywood, add the inner sheet, and trim edges level. Remember, the inner plywood stops at the frame ends, but the outer plywood projects.

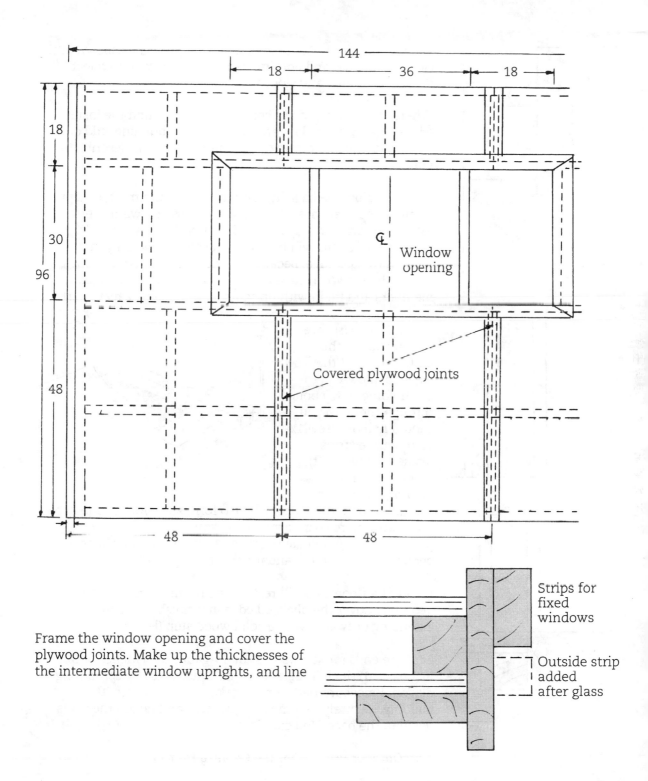

144

18 — 36 — 18

18

30

96

48

C̵L

Window opening

Covered plywood joints

48 — 48

Frame the window opening and cover the plywood joints. Make up the thicknesses of the intermediate window uprights, and line

Strips for fixed windows

Outside strip added after glass

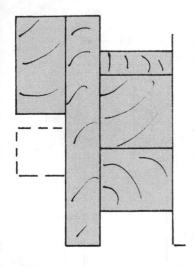

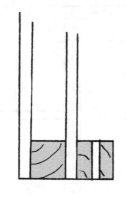

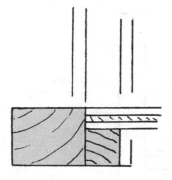

all openings (left). The lining pieces can project as shown at the sides. At the top and bottom, you can let the wood project further outwards and slope to shed water.

Where the fixed windows come, put strips round the inside edge. When you fit glass after erecting the building, add outside strips. Making and fitting the opening window is described later.

You will make the back in a similar way to the front, except it is lower and there are no windows, unless you want them. Allow the same overlaps at the joints with the shed ends. Check that heights will match at the corners when you have beveled the top edge. Because the back is covered without breaks, have two or three intermediate full-length horizontal members and fill in with uprights spaced about 2 feet apart.

No framing parts are exposed along the bottom edge of the walls to allow you to put holding-down bolts through them, so you should nail or screw 1½-inch-square strips inside all walls (left), and use them for holding down. With

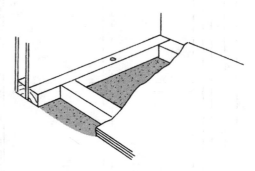

this all around, the strips will also form supports for a plywood floor, with more strips arranged across. If you use ¾-inch plywood for the floor, supports at 16-inch centers will be enough and will suit standard sheet sizes (right).

If you fit a floor, this will rest on the framing piece below the doorway. Cover the plywood edge and finish space by extending outwards with a solid wood step (left).

Drill the ends for screws—12- or 14-gauge by 3 inches or 3½ inches, at 12-inch intervals. Check squareness by comparing diagonal measurements or floor panels as you erect the building. Securely join the shed corners and fasten the walls down to the base. You can fit the floor now or later.

Cover the corner joints with upright side pieces, then with pieces overlapping them on the ends. These improve appearance and protect the plywood edges from the risk of water entering end grain.

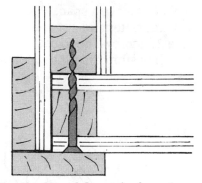

Roof

If the roof is to overhang 6 inches at back and front, its length is more than that of a standard plywood sheet, so you will have to join. Arrange rafters to suit the 4-foot width of standard sheets with a 6-inch overhang at the ends (below)

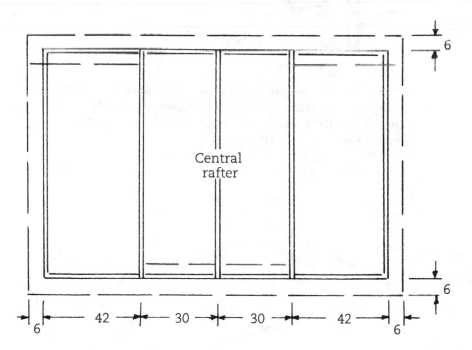

Central rafter

6

6

6   42   30   30   42   6

This will leave a space 5 feet wide, so you will have to fit a central rafter and cut sheets to 30 inches wide to fill the gap. Use 2-inch-by-3-inch section wood for the rafters and provide notched supports at their ends (below).

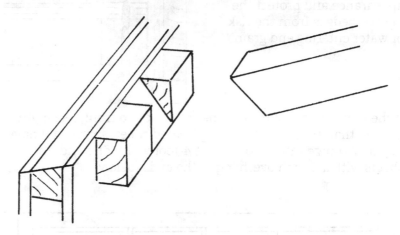

You will have to lengthen standard 8-foot sheets by about 12 inches. Do this with joint covers 6 inches wide underneath, glued and either screwed or clench-nailed (below). Cut the covers to fit between rafters.

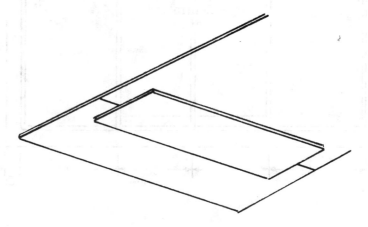

Nail the plywood roof to the rafters and the walls. While you will still want to fit the parts closely, the joints will be waterproofed by the tarred felt or other covering material. Cover the roof in the same way as described for the previous two projects.

Make the door with similar plywood and framing to the walls, but use solid wood edging all around (below). Thicken for strength at the hinge points and where you intend to fit a lock or catch. Allow for the door having easy clearance above the step and a working clearance round the edges. Hinges can be let into the door edges, with screws long enough to go into the internal framing.

Door

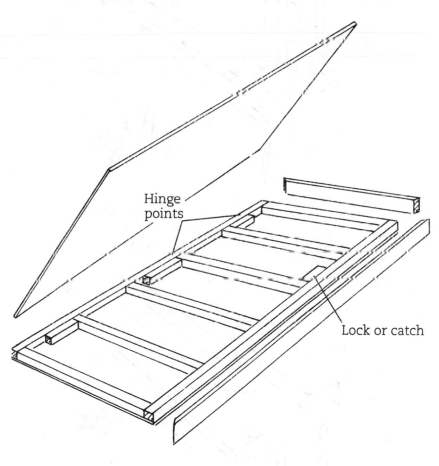

Hinge points

Lock or catch

You can fit a strip the full height of the doorway on the opening side to act as a stop. You could continue similar strips across the top and down the other side as draft-proofing.

Windows When you put the glass in the fixed windows between the strips, you can bed the glass edges in putty or jointing compound to keep rainwater out.

The opening window closes against similar rear stops (below), which go all around for weatherproofing.

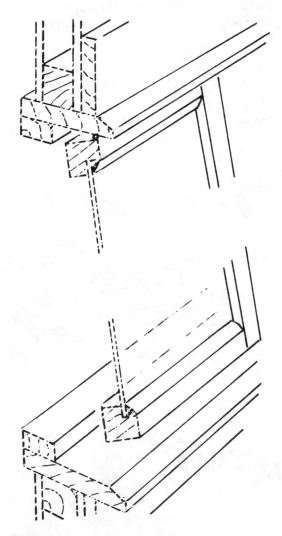

194 Outdoor Projects for the Country Home

You have to rabbet the window frame and make strong joints. A suitable rabbet is suggested (shown at right), but you might be able to buy window framing already close to this section.

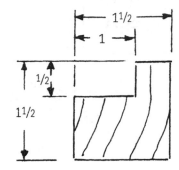

Corner joints should be tenoned (below left), with tenons on the horizontal members. Leave some extra length on the mortised parts until after assembly, to prevent grain breaking out (below right).

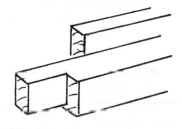 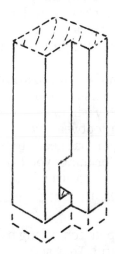

Make the window to fit easily. Hinge it at the top and provide a strut or stay at the bottom to adjust the amount of opening. Fit the glass with a few pins and putty.

If the external plywood is to have a long life, it should be adequately protected with paint. The border and joint strips could be a different color to give a distinctive appearance. Use a finish on the roof to suit the covering material, probably bitumastic paint.

Final touches

You might choose to leave the inside untreated, but a light color gives a roomy appearance and improves lighting. Linoleum or similar floor covering is comfortable to your feet and kind to edge tools that might fall on the floor. In addition, a plain-colored floor makes it easy to find anything small you drop.

PROJECT
1

Around the house

BECAUSE YOUR COUNTRY HOME INCLUDES A HOUSE AS WELL AS SOME LAND, you have to relate house to property and, at some stages, consider them together. This is not a book about making things for use inside the house, but you will probably have a deck or patio or a path connecting house and land. You can make a few things from wood that will come in handy in this in-between ground.

You might want to arrange displays of flowers or plants in containers to supplement what is growing in the ground. You probably will have to deal with changing from outdoor to indoor footwear. When the weather is wet, mud can be a problem that needs to be kept at bay. This chapter offers a few ideas for things you can make to solve these problems. Maybe the projects given here will start you thinking with ideas of your own.

Plant container

Plain pots containing plants or flowers are utilitarian, but not beautiful. They serve their purpose very well, but your display will look more attractive if the pot is hidden inside a wooden container.

The container shown on the facing page uses waney-edge wood, so the uneven edge provides part of the decoration. You can make the container with straight-edge boards, or you can cut the extended edges unevenly to get a wavy effect.

The drawing (below right) shows a container to take a pot 12 inches diameter and 12 inches high, but you could vary sizes to suit your needs. The pot does not have to be a close fit inside. Suggested wood is 1 inch thick, and a surface straight from the saw will probably look better than planed wood for this project.

Materials

4 sides	$1 \times 14 \times 16$
4 rims	$1 \times 3 \times 18$
1 bottom	$1 \times 18 \times 18$

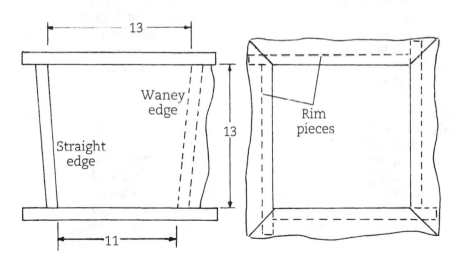

Waney edge

Straight edge

13

11

13

Rim pieces

All four sides are the same. The straight side of a piece butts against its neighbor and the waney edge extends. You will have to judge how much to let that edge project, according to how wavy it is, but 2 inches is about right.

Nail these pieces together squarely. Make the rim pieces with straight inner edges level with the inside of the box. Make the waney outer edges all about 3 inches wide. Miter the corners, and nail to the box sides. Remove sharpness from the corners.

Make the bottom to extend about the same size as the top. You will probably have to make this up from two or more boards. Drill a few ½-inch holes near the center of the bottom to provide drainage, and nail the bottom to the sides. If you want to stand the container on uneven ground, nail on 3-inch-square blocks under the corners to act as feet.

A single container is attractive, but two or more with matching foliage, as shown on page 197, will increase the effect.

Display stand

Your collection of potted plants and flowers can be displayed attractively on shelves at different levels. You could arrange the shelves in steps in many ways, but the suggested design (shown on facing page) is tapered in width so you can arrange pots over a wider area on the lowest shelf and floor, then decrease the width with higher displays, possibly giving special plants more prominence. A row of similar small plants could serve as a basic feature, leading to one or more choice plants higher up.

Materials

4 uprights	1 x 2 x 28	4 slats	1 x 2 x 20
2 uprights	1 x 2 x 20	4 slats	1 x 2 x 36
2 uprights	1 x 2 x 10	4 slats	1 x 2 x 50
2 rails	1 x 2 x 38	1 stay	1 x 2 x 18
2 rails	1 x 2 x 26	1 stiffener	1 x 5 x 36
2 rails	1 x 2 x 15	1 stiffener	1 x 5 x 22
2 braces	1 x 2 x 30	1 stiffener	1 x 5 x 14

This stand is made with the sides at about 60° to each other, so the top shelf widens from 12 inches and the lower shelf is 48 inches wide. Shelves rise in 9-inch steps. This arrangement should suit most displays, but you can vary sizes without altering the basic design.

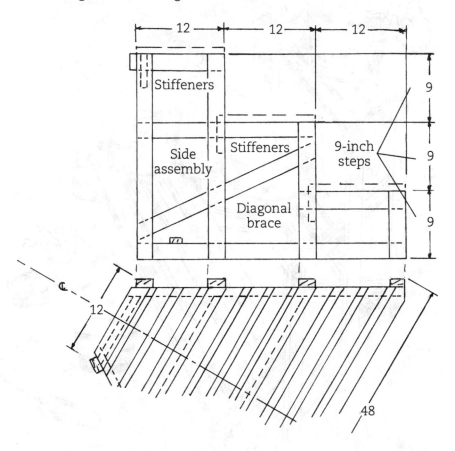

Nearly all parts are 1-inch-by-2-inch-section wood. Construction is almost entirely nailed, but waterproof glue in the joints would be an advantage. Use screws to join the transverse stiffeners to their shelves.

Start by making a pair of side assemblies. All uprights are outside. Cut the top rails to extend 1 inch, and trim these ends after fitting the shelf slats. Check squareness, and fit the diagonal braces to hold the parts in shape. See that the assemblies match each other.

Make a temporary assembly with strips across at the top rear and the bottom front, and in the bottom stay position. While it is on a level surface, adjust the stand to get it symmetrical. Add some of the shelf slats at all levels to hold the side assemblies in place. Remove the temporary strips, and complete the fitting of shelf slats at all levels. See that the structure is vertical as you fit the bottom stay.

To give rigidity crosswise, there are 5-inch-deep stiffeners attached to the backs of the lower shelves and under the top shelf. Cut the ends to fit against the uprights.

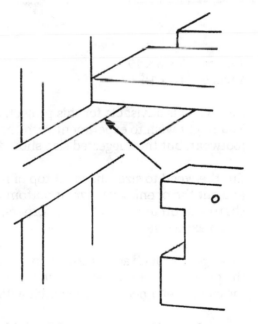

You can expect the stand to be wet more often than it's dry, from moisture draining from the pots and from rain, so you should probably treat the wood with preservative. You might prefer to paint it if you want to match other woodwork, but paint would need frequent renewing, and you would have to watch for the onset of rot.

Boot jack

Outdoor footwear, particularly rubber boots, are often difficult to remove, especially when coated with mud. A simple jack allows you to remove boots without using your hands (shown below). You simply put the heel of the boot to be removed in the V opening. Then hold down the end with your other foot, while you pull the foot out of the gripped boot.

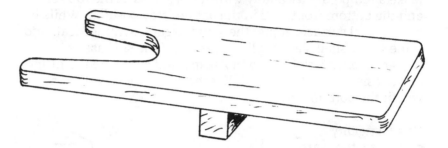

Materials

1 piece   ¾ × 6 × 19
1 piece   1½ × 1½ × 7

Hardwood is advisable for this project. Sizes are not crucial. You might wish to experiment with the opening to suit your footwear, but the suggested size should suit most heels.

Cut the wood to size (shown at top of facing page), and mark and cut the opening (shown at bottom of facing page). Take sharpness off and round outer corners, but do not round the notch excessively.

Arrange the block across so it is forward of the midpoint, then the greater weight at the back will keep that end down, ready for you to get a heel into the notch without adjusting.

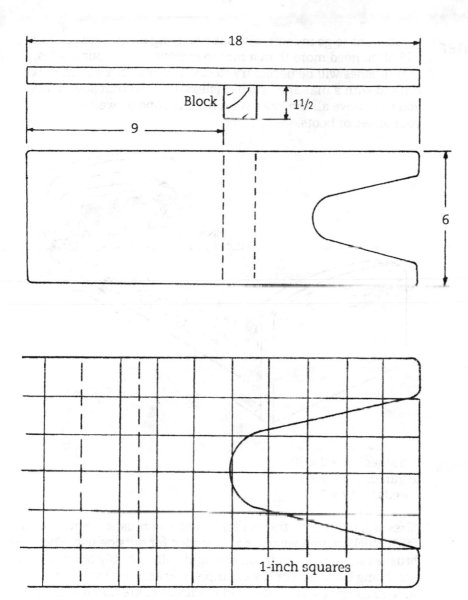

18

Block 1½

9

6

1-inch squares

Shoe cleaner

If you want to go indoors without removing dirty footwear, you will often need more than a mat to remove mud around soles: Stiff brushes will be necessary to clean the sides. You can make a stand with a mat and brushes (shown below) that should help you to remove all the loose mud from around as well as under your shoes or boots.

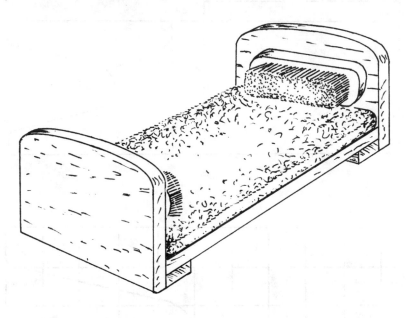

Materials

4 frames	1 × 2 × 20
2 frames	1 × 2 × 11
2 ends	¾ × 7 × 11

Sizes will depend on the available mat and brushes. You need a fairly thick, coarse-weave mat intended for outside use. The brushes should have stiff bristles and will probably be sold as scrubbing brushes. For the example, it is assumed you have a mat 10 inches by 18 inches and the brushes are about 8 inches long.

You could use softwood throughout, although it would be stronger to have hardwood sides. You will get better results by joining with screws instead of nails.

Make the bottom frame (shown below) slightly longer than the mat. The gaps between slats allow dirt from the mat to fall through. The ends should be high enough to take the brushes. Curve the tops and round the edges. You could extend one or both ends upward and cut slots for hand grips if you expect to vary the location of the cleaner.

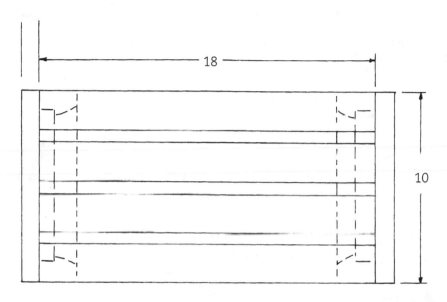

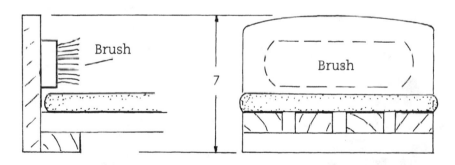

Brush

Brush

Screw through the sides into the brushes, giving them a little clearance above the mat. Finish the woodwork with paint. A bright color might draw attention to the cleaner and encourage reluctant shoe-wipers to use it.

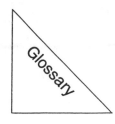

The making of wooden items for your country property or homestead is only part of the much wider craft of woodworking. The selection of words that follows includes some that are particularly appropriate to the subject of this book and might be helpful to readers unfamiliar with this branch of the craft.

anchor bolt bolt set in concrete with its thread end projecting.

apex the top, particularly of a roof.

ark a building for animals, usually A-shaped.

bargeboards covering boards at the gable end of a roof.

battens strips of wood of light section, such as are used on a roof to hold down the covering.

bay a space or section in a building.

beam horizontal load-carrying member in any structure.

butt fit against another piece. The end of a log or post.

carriage bolt bolt with shallow domed head and square neck to grip wood. Also called coach bolt.

cladding the covering of boards that forms the outside of a wall.

clapboarding overlapping boards, usually tapered in section, and used as cladding.

coach bolt alternative name for carriage bolt.

coop small house for poultry.

dibbler, dibber tool for making holes in ground for planting bulbs etc.

drawknife broad cutting tool with handles at ends for cutting by pulling.

eaves the angle between roof and wall. Overhang of roof over a wall. Never spelled without the s, even if there is only one.

exterior-grade plywood weather-resistant plywood bonded with waterproof glue.

feather edge wood tapered in section so one edge is thin.

foxiness first signs of rot.

froe knife-edge tool with lever handle for splitting wood.

gable end of a roof, usually one with a ridge.

gusset covering piece to make joint between two or more parts.

handed made as a pair.

haft a straight handle, as on a hammer.

hurdle portable section of fence, often made like a gate.

hutch house for small animals, such as rabbits.

jack lifting device. Helping equipment such as boot jack.

jamb upright side of doorway.

joist a supporting beam, as in a floor.

kerf the groove left when a saw cuts.

ledger crosswise member, particularly on a door. Also called ledge.

lintel support for a load over a doorway or other opening.

nominal when applied to lumber, this is the sawn size. Wood finished by machine planing will have smaller sections.

paling upright piece on a fence. Also called picket.

picket   alternative name for paling.

pilot hole   small hole drilled to check direction before enlarging to the required size.

pitch   slope of a roof. Distance between tops of a screw thread.

pop hole   hole in door or wall for poultry to pass through.

purlin   lengthwise support for roof covering, usually supported on rafters.

rabbet   recess in edge of wood, as in a picture frame. Also called *rebate*.

rafter   support for a roof.

rail   horizontal structural member.

ridge   the apex of a roof when made like an inverted V.

rive   to split wood deliberately.

roof truss   braced framework with rafters for supporting a roof.

season   to dry newly felled wood to an acceptable moisture level.

shake   lengthwise, naturally formed crack in wood.

sheathing   outside covering, such as cladding on a building.

shiplap boards   cladding boards to be laid horizontally, with the upper edge of each one fitting into a rabbet in the one above.

siding   the material used for cladding or sheathing.

sill   projecting horizontal board, as at the bottom of a window, to shed water away from the wall below. Also spelled *cill*.

slat   narrow strip of thin wood.

span   distance, particularly width of a roofed building.

stable door door in two parts, so you can open the top part while the lower part remains closed. Not necessarily on a stable.

stud vertical support in a wall.

template (templet) wood cut to desired outline and used for marking shapes, particularly when they have to be repeated.

tie member under tension in a structure, as across a roof truss, where it prevents rafters spreading.

tines teeth, as in a rake.

tongue-and-groove boards prepared so a tongue on the edge of one piece fits in a groove in the edge of the next piece.

trellis strips of wood arranged across each other to form a pattern of diamond openings. Used for decoration or to support climbing plants.

triangulation dividing a framework into triangles, as when placing a member diagonally across a four-sided figure, so it keeps its shape.

truss framed support, as in a roof truss.

vent an arrangement in a roof or wall to provide ventilation.

waney edge the shape of the outside of a tree retained on the edge of a board that has not been squared.

weatherboarding cladding boards to be laid horizontally, tapered in the width so the thin edge of a lower board goes under the thicker edge of the board above.

wicket gate small gate intended only for pedestrians and usually covered with upright palings.

wind bracing diagonal bracing arranged in the roof between gable, trusses, and purlins to resist distorting loads in the roof due to strong winds.

ALL THUMBS Guide to Painting, Wallpapering, and Stenciling —Robert W. Wood

Make your home look beautiful with a fresh coat of paint or new wallpaper. Wood shows you how to add a decorative touch to any or all rooms in the house. You'll learn how to patch holes in drywall, choose the right paint or wallpaper, apply the paper and clean up, use stencils for dramatic effect, and choose and use the tools of the trade. This helpful guide gives you easy-to-follow, step-by-step instructions, clear, how-to line drawings for each step . . . a convenient lay-flat binding . . . detachable tip cards with safety precautions, troubleshooting steps, and shopping lists . . . and an all-inclusive glossary of terms. 144 pages, 180 illustrations. Book No. 4060, $9.95 paperback only

ALL THUMBS Guide to Repairing Major Home Appliances —Robert W. Wood

Fix that broken washing machine, and tackle many other jobs. This helpful guide gives you easy-to-follow,; step-by-step in-structions, clear, how-to line drawings for each step . . . a convenient lay-flat binding, detachable tip cards with safety precautions, troubleshooting steps, and shopping lists, and an all-inclusive glossary of terms. It clearly explains how home appliances work and how to remedy typical problems. With the exploded-view drawings and step-by-step instructions, you'll get all the support you need to disassemble, repair, and re-assemble common electrical appliances, such as electric heaters, clothes washers and dryers, and dishwashers. 144 pages, 180 illustrations. Book No. 4061, $9.95 paperback only

FROM RAMSHACKLE TO RESALE: Fixing Up Old Houses for Profit —Carol Boyle

This book includes extensive guidelines that show you how to identify and recycle properties quickly and inexpensively. With no experience, little cash, and this book, you can successfully convert an eyesore into an asset. Using the expert instruction provided, you will confidently progress through the stages of inspector, electrician, plumber, painter, carpenter, and interior designer to real estate broker. 304 pages, 192 illustrations. Book No. 3162, $15.95 paperback only

THE COMPLETE BOOK OF HOME INSPECTION—2nd Edition— Norman Becker, P.E.

Evaluate a property inside and out. To find problems when inspecting a new home or when maintaining your present home, consult this valuable guide for advice that's guaranteed to take the guesswork and stress out of home inspection for the buyer and the owner. Now updated to cover current building materials, construction techniques, and home heating, electrical, and plumbing systems, it walks you through every square inch of a house and shows you how to determine the soundness of its many components. 288 pages, 155 illustration. Book No. 4100, $12.95 paperback only

Bestsellers of Related Interest

FENCES, DECKS, AND OTHER BACKYARD PROJECTS —3rd Edition—Dan Ramsey

Transform your backyard living space from the ordinary into the extraordinary with this fantastic idea book. Packed with step-by-step instructions and hundreds of illustrations, this updated guide shows you how to choose, design, prepare, build, and maintain all types of beautiful fences, decks, and other outdoor structures. Veteran how-to author Dan Ramsey offers a veritable bonanza of backyard building ideals. 288 pages, Over 300 illustrations. Book No. 4071, $14.95 paperback, $24.95 hardcover

PLAYHOUSES, GAZEBOS and SHEDS—Percy W. Blandford

Build a workshop or playhouse in your backyard—and save hundreds of dollars by doing it yourself! All you need is a few basic tools and materials and *Playhouses, Gazebos and Sheds*! Detailed illustrations, step-by-step instructions, complete materials lists, and expert tips make this a one-stop guide, no matter what your skill level. Blandford's clear and conversational writing style will guide you through even the largest of outdoor building projects with ease. 150 pages, 200 illustrations. Book No. 4077, $9.95 paperback only

Prices Subject to Change Without Notice.

Look for These and Other TAB Books at Your Local Bookstore

To Order Call Toll Free 1-800-822-8158
(24-hour telephone service available.)

or write to TAB Books, Blue Ridge Summit, PA 17294-0840.

Title	Product No.	Quantity	Price

☐ Check or money order made payable to TAB Books

Charge my ☐ VISA ☐ MasterCard ☐ American Express

Acct. No. _____ Exp. _____

Signature: _____

Name: _____

Address: _____

City: _____

State: _____ Zip: _____

Subtotal	$	_____
Postage and Handling ($3.00 in U.S., $5.00 outside U.S.)	$	_____
Add applicable state and local sales tax	$	_____
TOTAL	$	_____

TAB Books catalog free with purchase; otherwise send $1.00 in check or money order and receive $1.00 credit on your next purchase.

Orders outside U.S. must pay with international money in U.S. dollars drawn on a U.S. bank.

TAB Guarantee: If for any reason you are not satisfied with the book(s) you order, simply return it (them) within 15 days and receive a full refund.

BC